THE COMPLETE GUIDE TO YORKIPOOS

Jordan Honeycutt

LP Media Inc. Publishing

Text copyright © 2020 by LP Media Inc.

All rights reserved.

No part of this book may be reproduced or transmitted in any form or by any means, electronic or mechanical, including photocopying, recording, or by an information storage and retrieval system – except by a reviewer who may quote brief passages in a review to be printed in a magazine or newspaper – without permission in writing from the publisher. For information address LP Media Inc. Publishing, 3178 253rd Ave. NW, Isanti, MN 55040

www.lpmedia.org

Publication Data

Yorkipoos

The Complete Guide to Yorkipoos – First edition.

Summary: "Successfully raising a Yorkipoo Dog from puppy to old age" – Provided by publisher.

ISBN: 978-1-952069-86-4

[1. Yorkipoo Dogs – Non-Fiction] I. Title.

This book has been written with the published intent to provide accurate and author-itative information in regard to the subject matter included. While every reasonable precaution has been taken in preparation of this book the author and publisher expressly disclaim responsibility for any errors, omissions, or adverse effects arising from the use or application of the information contained inside. The techniques and suggestions are to be used at the reader's discretion and are not to be considered a substitute for professional veterinary care. If you suspect a medical problem with your dog, consult your veterinarian.

Design by Sorin Rădulescu

First paperback edition, 2020

Cover Photo of "Maggie Mae" submitted by Nancy Coogan. Photo taken by Amanda Leichner of Serenity Pet Services: Yuma, AZ

TABLE OF CONTENTS

CHAPTER 14

CHAPTER 15

CHAPTER 16

CHAPTER 1
Breed History

What Is a Yorkipoo?

T he Yorkipoo is not a breed of its own right yet, but that doesn't keep it from stealing hearts across America and the world. A cross between a Yorkshire Terrier and either a Toy or Miniature Poodle, this lovable little ball of fur has a zest for life and an intelligent mind, making him perfectly suited to be a lifetime companion just about anywhere life takes you.

Photo Courtesy Minette Ocampo

History of the Yorkipoo

The origins of the Yorkipoo are largely unknown, as this crossbreed only dates back to about the early 2000s. After the introduction of other Poodle hybrid dogs, such as the Labradoodle and the Cockapoo, in the United States, there was a need for a dog with similar hypoallergenic qualities and intelligence in a smaller size.

To better understand the Yorkipoo, let's take a look at the crossbreed's parents of origin. Bred from a Yorkshire Terrier and a Toy Poodle, this dog can take on the character traits of either breed.

Yorkshire Terrier – A young breed itself, the Yorkshire Terrier is thought to have been developed around 100 years ago in Yorkshire, England. The Yorkshire Terrier is derived from the Scottish Waterside Terrier and was originally called the "Broken-haired Scotch Terrier" for nine years until the breed had improved enough to gain its own name, the Yorkshire Terrier.

Originally bred for hunting rats in mines, the version of the Yorkshire Terrier we have today is a bit smaller and not known for hunting, but still retains the breed's characteristic energy and enthusiasm.

Toy Poodle – Although the Poodle is the national dog of France, the breed actually originated in Germany as a duck hunter. Due to the Poodle's excellent trainability and flashy looks, this breed was prized in noble households in Europe and eventually became a well-known part of the European circus.

The Toy Poodle was bred down in size from the Standard Poodle in the early 20th century in America in order to adapt the beloved breed to better suit city dwellers. Although the Toy Poodle is now more of a lap and companion dog, the breed still retains the superior intelligence and swimming abilities of its ancestors.

Physical Characteristics

Because the Yorkipoo is a crossbreed, it is not recognized by the American Kennel Club and no breed standard exists. Due to the breed's very short history, most Yorkipoos are produced by breeding a Toy Poodle to a Yorkshire Terrier, resulting in a first-generation Yorkipoo. For these reasons, Yorkipoos can vary in appearance greatly from breeder to breeder. Although there is no standard, there are a few key features that are typically present in a Yorkipoo.

Yorkipoos are a very small breed and typically only stand between 7 and 9 inches tall and weighing 7 to 11 pounds. Yorkipoos will often (but not always) inherit the Poodle's long legs and fine bone structure. Although thin, Yorkipoos typically have a muscular build.

Photo Courtesy
of Bianca Jacques

The coat of the Yorkipoo comes in many varieties and can be anything from straight and silky to curly. Since the Poodle can produce a wide variety of coat colors, the Yorkipoo can appear in almost any color combination and markings you can imagine. White, Black, Sable, Red, Cream and Apricot are the most common colors seen on a Yorkipoo.

Typical Breed Behavior

Just as with the Yorkipoo's appearance, there is no breed standard for behavior. However, given what we know about the Toy Poodle and the Yorkshire Terrier, we can predict general breed behavior possibilities.

Yorkipoos are loving and affectionate to their owners and relish their time in the spotlight. Bred solely for companion purposes, the Yorkipoo is heavily dependent on his owner for interaction and will suffer greatly if left alone for any period of time.

Although they typically come around to befriend everyone they meet, Yorkipoos make excellent watchdogs and will bark to alert the entire neighborhood of an impending visitor.

The Terrier side of this hybrid dog gives the Yorkipoo its high energy and bold nature, one that comes as a shock to many coming from a dog of this size. The Poodle contributes to the breed's high intelligence and excellent trainability. Eager to please their owners, Yorkipoos are highly responsive to praise when training and typically will perform just to be the star of the show.

Many Yorkipoo owners are tempted to treat these pint-sized pooches as living dolls, dressing them up and catering to their every need. While this may be fun, it can often cause your Yorkipoo to believe he is the "king of the castle," leading to a somewhat tyrannical pattern of behavior. These dogs may be small, but they have the spirit of a breed ten times its size and can cause quite a bit of a headache for owners if not trained properly.

FUN FACT
First-timers

Yorkipoos were rated in the top fifteen dog breeds and hybrids recommended for first-time pet owners by Dogtime. com in 2020. Listed among their attributes were their easygoing nature and confidence.

4

Photo Courtesy of Lynn Scarborough

Is a Yorkipoo the Right Choice for You?

"Yorkipoos are highly versatile little dogs who love to be an active part of their human family. A family with an active life style that includes their fur baby is the best suited for owning a Yorkipoo."

JENNIFER EMERT
Jen's Tiny Toys

If you're looking for a beautiful, pint-sized dog that offers love, affection, and endless spunk, the Yorkipoo is the right dog for you! Compact and adaptable, Yorkipoos can live anywhere. This includes apartments, houses with yards, or even recreational vehicles for the most adventurous travel types.

Yorkipoos offer friendship to those they know best and can do well with children if introduced properly. Children can benefit greatly from caring for a dog, but they must be trained to properly handle a Yorkipoo due to the dog's small and fragile size. The feisty, yet friendly nature of these dogs helps them play the role of family pet with energetic passion, but it is worth considering that small children can sometimes injure smaller dogs and puppies unintentionally with extra tight hugs or too-firm pats. Always teach your children to be gentle so they don't accidentally injure your Yorkipoo.

Though they require less physical exercise than a larger breed of dog, Yorkipoos require more than average time with their owners and have high grooming needs. Companionship and care is of utmost importance for the breed and your dog will suffer if he does not receive it.

Although the Yorkipoo is generally healthier than his pure-bred counterparts, there are some health issues that affect both the Yorkshire Terrier and the Poodle. This is something you should be prepared to handle before stepping into dog ownership. These health conditions will be discussed in greater detail in Chapter 13.

Before bringing your Yorkipoo home, it's important to carefully consider all aspects of ownership. Taking on a dog of any breed presents challenges and frustrations. Can you afford to care for your dog? Do you have the time to devote to it? Are there any restrictions where you live? If you are willing to properly prepare for the dog you choose, the transition into dog parenthood should be a smooth one.

CHAPTER 2
Choosing Your Yorkipoo

Buying vs. Adopting

Deciding whether to purchase your Yorkipoo from a breeder or adopt from a rescue can be a tough decision. We all have our heartstrings plucked when we see commercials showing dogs in need but oftentimes these dogs have special needs, medical or social, and require a special kind of home. If you think you can provide the patience and care it may take

Photo Courtesy
of Michelle Quier

7

to adopt a rescue Yorkipoo, please do so! The dog will reward you with love and companionship just as much as one you raise from a puppy.

One key benefit to adopting an older Yorkipoo is having the chance to learn the dog's personality before you bring him home. You'll know ahead of time if the dog enjoys the company of young children or other dogs, what level of exercise this particular dog expects, and exactly how to handle any medical or social issues he may have. There are very few surprises when it comes to adopting a well-established, older Yorkipoo.

A rescue dog often seems to show a special appreciation for a new chance at a forever home. If you're looking to adopt a Yorkipoo and happen to find one at a rescue, chances are the dog will be adopted fast, so don't hesitate to get your application in!

Importance of Breeder Reputation

"When researching your breeder, visit the kennel to meet the parent dogs and see how the puppies are raised. Check the health of the parents, both physical & mental - are they happy? Are they and the puppies socialized with people and other dogs (other than just their mother)? Are they friendly? How do the puppies react when they are picked up, held, and placed in a new area? Are they shy & hide or do they look around to investigate?"

MARY LISA CARTER
Sunny Day Puppies

If you choose the breeder route, finding a trustworthy breeder can be challenging when there are so many questionable breeders out there. People will pay good money for a "designer" crossbred dog, and this has caused many to take up what is commonly called backyard breeding. These breeders often do little or no testing to ensure the health of their litters. Some of these places even turn out to be puppy mills, where dogs are kept alive to do nothing more than pump out litter after litter. The dogs are often kept in small cages and in unclean conditions. This is a terrible life for a dog! Avoiding supporting places like this is just as important as ensuring the health of your puppy.

A good, reputable breeder will be known as such in the Yorkipoo breeder community. They will undoubtedly have connections with other reputable breeders. If you find a good breeder who has no current available puppies, you may want to contact them and ask for the names of other breeders in the area. A reputable breeder is always concerned with breeding healthy dogs and should only recommend the same.

Photo Courtesy
of Colleen Thomas

Finding the Right Breeder

The internet makes finding a reputable breeder easier than ever and yet challenging at the same time. If you do a quick internet search for "Yorkipoo puppies for sale," you will find a whole slew of breeders. Some of these, no doubt, you will want to avoid. How can you tell the difference between a reputable breeder and someone who is just trying to make a quick buck without any care for the well-being of the dogs?

CELEBRITY YORKIPOOS

Dogs in the Senate

US Senator Roy Blunt of Missouri is often accompanied by his son's Yorkipoo named Max. Roy says, "Max may be small, but he has a big personality. As soon as we get into the office, he sprints off to find someone to pet him or give him a belly rub. He's pretty shameless about seeking attention. Luckily, he fares well with staff and visitors. No matter how tough or busy the day gets, Max puts everyone in a good mood."

Health Tests and Certifications

There are several questions you should ask any breeder when you are searching for the perfect Yorkipoo puppy.

Can I Visit the Breeding Facility? The answer to this question should always be a resounding yes. A breeder might not allow you into certain areas of the facility for the safety of the puppies. There is a concern of tracking in diseases that could be detrimental to a young puppy's undeveloped immune system. However, a quality breeder should always allow you to come on-site and see other dogs in their program. If they refuse, this could be a sign they have something to hide, and you should reconsider.

How Long Have You Been Breeding Yorkipoos? The answer to this question should be several years. You should only buy from an experienced breeder who is well established. A quality breeder who has several years of experience will know all the ins and outs of breeding for only the most desirable traits and healthy dogs.

What Genetic Conditions Do You Test for Before Breeding and What Conditions Do You Screen the Puppies for Before Selling? There are numerous genetic conditions that Poodles and Yorkshire Terriers are prone to developing, which are discussed in detail in Chapter 13. Before agreeing to purchase a puppy, ask for a detailed list of the tests the breeder performed on the parents, and ask for copies of the test results. These tests should be performed by certified specialists for each potential ailment, such

Photo Courtesy
of Sheila Nelson

as a board-certified veterinarian cardiologist and an ophthalmologist. Just because the breeder had the dogs checked out by a general veterinarian does not mean they were genetically tested for undesirable traits.

Can I See Veterinary Records for Both Parents? When investing your time and money into a Yorkipoo puppy, you will want to have an open and transparent line of communication with your chosen breeder. If the breeder is not willing to share medical records of the puppy's parents, this may be a signal that you should find another breeder. Both the dam and the sire should have been checked by specialists and cleared for defects. The breeder should also provide proof of genetic testing.

What Kind of Guarantee Do You Provide for Your Puppies? A good breeder will always guarantee the health of their puppies. Look for guarantees that will refund most or all of the cost of the puppy in the event any congenital health conditions appear within the first year. Beware of breeders who only offer to replace the puppy with a healthy one with no option to receive a refund instead. If the breeder produced a genetically unhealthy puppy the first time, why would you want to bring home another puppy from the same place? Many people are also unwilling to return their dog for a replacement, as they have already become attached. This is a low-risk guarantee from a breeder and may be a warning sign. On the other hand, a responsible breeder will always take back a dog that you can no longer care for, no matter the reason.

Many times, a breeder's health guarantee will have stipulations. These may include not neutering or spaying until after a year so that the dog's joints are allowed to fully develop, feeding your puppy a proper diet, and regular visits to the vet. As much as a responsible breeder wants their puppies to remain in perfect health for their entire life, not all owners care for a dog the same way, and health results will vary based on lifestyle.

Remember, no matter how good the breeding lines are or how thorough the testing, no breeder can guarantee perfect health for a dog's entire life. If something does go wrong with your puppy, before putting the blame on the breeder, it is important to understand any role you may have unwittingly played in the situation.

Do You Ever Sell to a Broker or Pet Shop? If the answer is yes, walk away from this breeder immediately, and do not support them. A responsible breeder, breeding for the betterment of the dog's health and appearance, will never sell one of their animals to a broker or a pet store. Reputable breeders want to meet the families of each of their puppies to be sure they will be properly cared for. Puppies found in a pet shop are bred for profit alone and come with no health guarantee.

Breeder Contracts and Guarantees

A lot of breeders require buyers to sign a contract. It specifically outlines what is and is not acceptable to do with the dog. The average contract defines the payment amount for the Yorkipoo puppy and has terms or rules for what happens if you can no longer keep the dog. Most breeders require that you return the Yorkipoo to them instead of giving the dog to a rescue or surrendering it to the animal shelter.

Some breeder contracts also require that you spay or neuter your dog. There will often be a time requirement for this. As more research comes out, breeders are more often stipulating that you wait until after the dog is fully mature, between 12 and 18 months old, before sterilizing. This is said to help prevent certain diseases, including bone cancer.

Picking the Perfect Puppy

"Be honest with the breeder or rescue about your lifestyle and your needs. This will help them to match you to the correct Yorkipoo. Each one is different, and you will find yourself happiest if you allow the rescue and/or breeder to help you select the Yorkipoo with the right temperament for you."

JENNIFER EMERT
Jen's Tiny Toys

Although temperament and behavioral characteristics should be relatively consistent throughout a well-bred litter of Yorkipoos, this brand new cross-breed can produce puppies with a variety of personalities. Depending on generation and lineage, one puppy may take on more of a Poodle personality and another more of a Yorkshire Terrier. If possible, visit your breeder's facility to pick out your new puppy. Often, breeders have waiting lists of people hoping to purchase a puppy from their next litter. Once you have chosen a reputable breeder, it is important to get on the list as soon as possible. This will allow you the best possible chance of getting an early pick from the litter.

If you are able to visit the litter beforehand, there are a few things to keep in mind. If the puppies are all playing together, does one seem more aggressive than another? This kind of puppy may be feisty, energetic, and a bit more assertive by nature. Is there one who would rather play alone in the corner with its own toy? This puppy may be a bit more docile and independent. Is there one that is climbing all over you, gnawing on your

*Photo Courtesy
of Karri Meyers*

hands or shoes? This could be a puppy with a curious and adventurous personality. None of these personalities are better or worse than the other, but you should have a type of dog in mind that you are hoping for so that you can make the best choice for your family and for your future puppy.

If you are unsure which puppy you should choose, ask the breeder for help. They have spent the most time with the puppies and should have a good idea of each of their personalities.

Raising Multiple Puppies from the Same Litter

There are many reasons why some people consider bringing home two puppies at once. They may believe that the dogs can keep each other company while they're at work. They may want to get a puppy for each child. They may even decide to get two because they just can't pick between the dogs! While these may seem like valid reasons at first glance, you may want to reconsider.

Most experts warn against getting two puppies at the same time, especially from the same litter. The work of caring for one puppy is hard, but the work of caring for two puppies can easily be overwhelming. Each puppy will need to be crated, played with, and trained separately. There will be twice the mess and accidents to clean up, too.

It is true that the puppies will most likely grow up to be best friends. However, this often happens at the expense of the dog-owner relationship. The two dogs will create an inseparable bond that you cannot compete with.

A reputable breeder should always advise against getting two dogs at once. Most breeders will actually refuse to sell multiples unless you have proof that you can care for them both properly. If you really want to have two dogs, get them at different times. Start with one dog so you can establish a bond, and then if you want another, repeat the bonding process with that one before the two are allowed to pair up. This can be done by intentionally spending quality alone time with your new dog as often as possible. No matter how intentional you are, however, many people find that the two dogs will develop a bond that could potentially take away from the one shared between human and dogs.

The Different Puppy Personality Types

"Match your personality with your puppy. If you like being a little ornery then your puppy will also be ornery! However, don't think a Yorkipoo will be completely laid back because you are. That's not going to happen, they love to explore and play."

LINDA OSBORNE
Pocket Puppies

Most puppies fit into one of 5 categories.

The Dominant Puppy – This puppy could be bossy, pushy, and possibly more vocal than the others. He may be more rebellious and challenging to train. These puppies can potentially have behavior problems later in life if they aren't trained early.

The Active Puppy – Active puppies can be somewhat pushy and bossy and sometimes a little mouthy. They are typically high-energy dogs that get excited very easily. They can get easily distracted, which can make training more of a challenge.

The Affectionate Puppy – These puppies are friendly and eager to please. They learn new things rather quickly and are quite easy to train. Outgoing and self-confident, they are a wonderful choice for families with children. They tend to form extraordinarily strong bonds quickly with their humans. They generally get along well with other dogs and animals and are potentially more accepting of other pets than other personality types. These dogs are happiest near their companions.

The Calm Puppy – More submissive than others, the calm puppy is typically happy to be a follower. Such puppies can be quite affectionate. These dogs are eager to please but sometimes require more work to motivate during training. They are mostly friendly and get along well with other dogs and animals, but they can be prone to separation anxiety when left alone.

The Fearful Puppy – Highly submissive dogs, these puppies can be quite shy and timid at times and are easily scared or intimidated. They lack self-confidence and can be quite sensitive. These dogs do best when they have a calm and quiet owner who has compassion and patience. Loud noises, punishment, and even light corrections may be too much for these dogs to handle. A reputable Yorkipoo breeder should not have any fearful puppies in a healthy litter. Fearful puppies may be a red flag that something is wrong.

Tips for Adopting a Yorkipoo

If you have your heart set on adopting a Yorkipoo, there are a number of resources available to you. The internet is a great place to begin your search for local Yorkipoo Rescues. Yorkshire Terrier and Poodle mixes are frequently found right in your own local animal shelter. Call or visit these places and let them know what you are looking for. If they do not currently have a Yorkipoo ready for adoption, they may be willing to contact you if one comes into their facility.

The Difference Between Animal Shelters and Rescues

In the United States, there are three different classifications for pet and animal rescues: municipal shelters, no-kill shelters, and non-profit rescue organizations. It is important to know the differences and the benefits of each to help you better prepare in the search for your Yorkipoo.

Municipal Shelters – These shelters take in strays, abandoned animals, and animals surrendered by their owners. They are run and funded by local governments. The animals there have a limited time to be adopted along with an extremely high turnover rate, as the animals are usually euthanized due to lack of space.

These government-run shelters house their animals on-site in a kennel-like environment. Most of them have veterinarians on staff that supply basic medical care as well as spay and neuter operations. They have paid staff supplemented by volunteers who help care for the dogs and clean the facility. Adoption fees are typically low at these places. Almost all require an animal to be spayed or neutered before it is adopted.

Shelters are a great option for finding local pets in need of a home. These facilities are almost always fighting an overpopulation problem. If you adopt from a shelter, be aware that the stressful environment can cause a dog to act fearful or aggressive, even if that is not its true personality. This is known as "kennel syndrome." Ask if your shelter allows trial periods where you can take the dog home for a few days to see if he is a good match for your family. This will enable you to see him outside of the high-stress environment of the kennel.

No-Kill Shelters – These are private organizations that will not kill a healthy and adoptable animal. They have a limited intake policy and end up turning many animals away because they do not have the space to house them.

Dogs are often kept here for an extended time; months and sometimes even years go by before they are adopted. Foster homes are often used in these situations to allow the dog an opportunity to live in a home-like environment. Many times, this can help a troubled dog adjust and become more adoptable.

Non-Profit Rescue Organizations – These organizations are mostly run and operated by volunteers. They utilize foster houses to save as many animals as possible. They do not euthanize animals.

Typically privately funded or dependent on donations, many rescues are breed-specific and dedicated to saving one specific dog type, such as

Yorkipoos. Rescues often offer the same medical care and spay and neuter services as municipal shelters, but only a few have a veterinarian on staff. These rescues often pay full price for veterinary services, which becomes a significant expense.

Most rescue groups rely heavily on foster families. Some may not have a physical facility at all but instead maintain a website with information about their available and adoptable dogs. Because the dog lives with a foster family, more is known about the dog's history and personality, making it easier to find a compatible home.

Due to their higher costs, rescues usually have much higher adoption fees than shelters do. They also have much stricter adoption guidelines and policies, and some even require a home inspection before approval. Much like with a typical breeder, many have policies in place that require adopters to return the dog to the rescue if they can no longer keep the animal.

The rescue usually maintains contact with the adopter for 3-6 months after the adoption takes place. During this time, they may do another home inspection to ensure things are going well and that the dog is happy and healthy.

Keep in mind, dogs that find their way into rescue facilities often have experienced some kind of trauma. Sometimes they come with significant health issues, social issues, or even behavioral problems. Make sure you are prepared to handle the problems that may arise so that you and your adopted Yorkipoo can have the best life together possible.

CHAPTER 3
Preparing for Your Yorkipoo

Before bringing home your Yorkipoo, be sure to prepare your home and your family. Puppy pick-up day is exciting for everyone but there is nothing worse than getting your new puppy home and then realizing you are not quite ready for the new arrival! By taking the time to get everything in order before you bring home your puppy, the first few days with your new Yorkipoo will go much smoother.

Photo Courtesy
of Ruth Llewellyn

Preparing Children and Other Pets

If you are bringing your new puppy home to a house with no children or other pets, the transition should be a relatively easy one. If you do have children or other pets, you must make careful preparations to allow everyone time to adjust. In regards to children, depending on their age, the only preparations needed will be to teach them gentle handling of your future puppy. Most children are excited and cannot wait to get their new puppy, so adjusting them to the idea should be a breeze. Yorkipoos in general are delicately built dogs, so it is especially important to show children how to safely hold, pick up, and pet your puppy. Often, a small child can harm a puppy unintentionally by trying to show affection in a manner too rough. Careful supervision should always be maintained with small children and puppies.

YORKIPOOS IN BOOKS
Emma Lou

Emma Lou the Yorkie Poo – Breathing In The Calm, written by Kim Larkins, is a book about a little dog with some big worries. Emma Lou, along with a cast of characters such as Patrick the Pig and Caleb the Calico cat, learns to calm her body and mind with a set of new mindfulness techniques. Parents and children alike can learn to cope with their worries and practice mindfulness alongside Emma Lou with this book.

It may also be beneficial to remind children of new puppy basics, such as a puppy's love of chewing. Teach them to pick up their possessions at all times and never leave them unattended with your Yorkipoo. One mistake may leave his or her beloved stuffed animal reduced to shreds.

Consider introducing older children to dog-care chores. Allow them to help in all aspects of care, such as feeding, brushing, and exercising your dog. Not only will this help the dog bond with the children, but it will teach the children a great deal of responsibility when they come to realize this little life is depending on them for care.

When it comes to adjusting your current pets to the idea of a new puppy, things may get a little more complicated. Depending on the type of pets and their nature, the transition may be simple or it may take a little extra work.

If you have another dog or multiple, warming them up to the idea of a new puppy before the introduction is a good idea. Discuss this transition with your chosen breeder and see if they will allow you to pick up a blanket or a toy with the new puppy's scent on it. Introduce the blanket or toy to your current dog or dogs and allow them to become accustomed to the smell of another puppy in the house.

When you pick up your new puppy, have some-one help you with the first introduction. If possible, let your dogs meet your new puppy in a neutral area where your current pets will be less likely to be territorial. Because your puppy's immune sys-tem is not fully developed, you will not want to take your new puppy to a park or another public place, but you may consider let-ting the dogs meet briefly outside of the house in a less used area. Keep your dogs leashed but give them a bit of slack so they can greet the puppy. Keep a close eye on all parties during the introduction to ensure the safety of your new puppy. Keep the first meeting brief and then separate your dogs from

Photo Courtesy of Jen Berg

the new puppy so they do not overwhelm each other. After you see how they react to each other, you can slowly allow them to spend more time together until they are completely acclimated and coexisting in harmony.

If the dog you are introducing your new pup to is advanced in age, take care to pay him extra caution. Your older dog may be more receptive and easygoing about the new arrival or he may become stressed by the endless energy of your new Yorkipoo. Take your dog's cues and respect his place in the household. If you find him stressing, give him plenty of space and time alone to help him adjust.

If you are introducing your puppy to a resident cat, it's important to keep both your cat and your puppy safe by maintaining control of your puppy or by allowing them to meet while one animal is contained by a crate or another barrier. Allow them short, controlled interactions at quiet moments of the day until they are both calm around each other. Always allow your cat to escape to a place only he can go in order to keep him from becoming stressed. This may be a place off the ground, such as a cat tree or even a favorite spot on the furniture where your dog cannot reach.

A new puppy can be exciting and become the focal point of life for a while. Remember to show your other dogs and pets some extra attention and love so they know that they are still important members of the family.

Puppy-Proofing Your Home

One of the first things you should do in preparation for your new Yorkipoo is to puppy-proof your home. There are many seemingly ordinary things in your home that could prove hazardous to your new puppy.

Tuck Away or Remove Any Electrical Cords Within the Puppy's Reach. Puppies are curious little creatures who love to explore, oftentimes with their mouths. If you cannot remove all cords from your puppy's reach, you may want to invest in some cord protectors. These cord wraps usually come infused with bitter flavors to help deter your Yorkipoo from chewing. If you find you have a particularly stubborn chewer, you can spritz the cords with hot pepper spray to ensure the dog will not find the cord appealing anymore.

Invest in Fully Enclosed Trash Cans if You Do Not Have Them Already. Keeping the kitchen trash out of reach may be a no-brainer, but even the smaller trash cans around your bathrooms and office are tempting toys for an energetic and curious Yorkipoo. Sometimes a used cotton swab or a wad of paper is just too irresistible not to chew up.

Lock Away All Drugs, Chemicals, and Cleaning Supplies. If you tend to keep any medications in an area that your puppy may be able to reach, be sure to move those to a higher location such as a dedicated, locked medicine cabinet. As mentioned above, puppies explore everything with their mouths, and snatching a bottle or box of medication off the sofa table could prove to be fatal for your new puppy.

Also, move any chemicals, cleaning supplies, dish pods, or laundry detergents into an enclosed area, out of reach of your puppy. This includes any rat bait or poisons that your new puppy may find enticing. Even if these items are in an area of the house where your puppy will not be allowed, it only takes one escape for your new Yorkipoo to encounter something detrimental.

Watch Out for Poisonous House Plants. House plants may seem innocent, but some are poisonous and can cause serious issues for a nibbling puppy. Some common houseplants that are potentially dangerous for your new puppy are the corn plant, sago palm, aloe, and jade plant. To find a complete list of common plants which are poisonous to dogs, visit the ASPCA website.

If you do happen to have one of the plants on this list, you don't neces-sarily have to give it up. Find a place that you are certain is out of reach from your puppy and leave it there. House plants have wonderful health benefits for you and your new puppy, and as long as you are informed and aware of the dangers, you will be able to keep your new puppy safe.

Beware of Xylitol. Xylitol is considered a sugar alcohol and is commonly found in items throughout almost every household. As people become more and more aware of the dangers of added sugars, companies are turning to xylitol, an additive that tastes sweet but does not spike blood sugar and insulin levels like sugar. Xylitol can be found in almost anything but is com-monly found in chewing gum, mints, candies, toothpaste, and even peanut butter. Xylitol is highly toxic to dogs and can cause dangerously low blood sugar levels resulting in weakness, seizures, trembling, or even death. When

Photo Courtesy
of Nancy Coogan

dogs consume very high levels of xylitol, it may cause necrosis of the liver, which often leads to death.

Be sure to keep all purses and bags which may contain gum, candies, or toothpaste out of reach of your puppy at all times. Have a designated area for guests' bags so that they are not accidentally left within reach. Also, check all food labels for xylitol. Peanut butter is often recommended to give a dog medication but be sure to check that your peanut butter does not contain xylitol first.

Keep the Batteries Away. While you probably don't have random batteries lying around on the floor, you may have remotes or small electronic toys. If your puppy is able to get hold of a battery-operated remote or toy, he can chew them to expose the battery. Small button cell batteries are the most dangerous as they are small enough for your puppy to swallow. Swallowing a battery is a serious, life-threatening issue and can cause internal burns. Call the nearest emergency vet immediately if you suspect your puppy may have swallowed a battery.

Put Away Children's Toys. Children's toys are often made up of small pieces that are a choking hazard to your dog. Be especially careful with toys that contain magnets inside, as these pose an extra risk of internal damage when more than one is consumed.

Keep Toilets Closed. Many people use automatically refreshing toilet bowl cleaners attached to the bowl of their toilet. These can pose risks to a thirsty pup. Remove chemical cleaners from your toilet bowl, or make sure you always keep the lid down.

Set Up Puppy Gates. After you have puppy-proofed your entire house, designate a safe, common area of the house for your puppy to stay. Use puppy gates to block any doorways or staircases so that it will be easier for you to keep a close eye on your new Yorkipoo. Having already puppy-proofed the entire house, you can be sure that even if your dog makes a great escape into a room where he is not allowed, the dangerous items have all been removed.

It only takes one second for your new puppy to get into something that could cause it harm, so you must notify everyone in the house of all of the changes before your puppy comes home.

Dangerous Things Your Dog Might Eat

Although feeding your dog food from the table is not recommended, it is often difficult to resist that adorably fluffy face and those begging eyes looking up at you while you eat. If you do get the urge to toss your pup a little treat, be aware of what he can and cannot have. There are a number of foods, perfectly healthy for humans, that can cause illness or toxicity in dogs.

Chocolate – A crowd favorite among humans, chocolate can cause major issues for your loving Yorkipoo. Chocolate contains methylxanthine, which is a stimulant that can stop a dog's metabolic process. Methylxanthines are found in especially high amounts in pure dark chocolate and baker's chocolate. Too much methylxanthine causes seizures and irregular heart function, which can lead to death.

Xylitol – As discussed above, xylitol is particularly dangerous to dogs as it does not take much to cause a dangerous or deadly reaction. Vomiting is typically the initial symptom of xylitol poisoning. If you suspect there is a chance your dog has ingested even a small amount of xylitol, call the veterinarian immediately because time is critical.

Raw or Cooked Bones – Raw or cooked bones are a choking hazard for your dog. The bones can break or splinter and become lodged or, worse, puncture their digestive tract. This is especially true with cooked bones of any kind, as they become dry and brittle. Pork and poultry bones are especially dangerous as they are more likely to splinter and cause issues.

Though controversial, some veterinarians say that raw bones of the right variety can provide healthy nutrients and help prevent tartar and plaque build-up in the mouth. These bones are recommended only under very close supervision and only for a few minutes at a time, keeping the bone in the refrigerator for a maximum of four days before discarding. If the bone is breaking or if your dog seems to be swallowing any pieces, discard the bone immediately. If you prefer to skip the risk, look for bones in the pet store that are meant to withstand the chewing power of a pint-sized Yorkipoo.

Other foods that may cause gastrointestinal upset or worse for your dog are grapes and raisins, certain nuts including macadamia nuts, avocados, apple cores, seeds, and anything in the allium family, including onions and garlic. This is not a comprehensive list, so it is best to check with your veterinarian before giving anything from your plate to your dog.

Supplies to Purchase Before You Bring Your Yorkipoo Home

Getting ready for a new dog can be overwhelming. There is so much information to learn and so many preparations to be made around the house. Gathering all the supplies you need before you bring your Yorkipoo home will make the first few days much easier for you and your puppy. Follow this list of essentials, and you will have all you need for the day you bring your dog home.

Food and Water Bowl – Food and water bowls come in many shapes, colors, and sizes. They can be made from ceramic, stainless steel, or plastic. When choosing a bowl set for your new puppy, there are a few things to consider. Plastic bowls may come in fun colors and patterns, but they are lightweight, easy to tip over, and many puppies think they are fun to chew on. They are also more difficult to clean when they become scratched or damaged.

Ceramic bowls are heavier, less likely to be tipped over, and they are easier to clean than plastic. They are breakable, though, so if your puppy does manage to knock a bowl over, it is likely to chip.

Stainless-steel bowls are both easy to clean and unbreakable, so even if a bowl is tipped over and kicked around, it should not be easily damaged. You can also buy bowls with wide rubber or silicone bases to stop sliding and prevent tipping.

Another option you will find in a pet store is an elevated bowl set. These are bowls that are set up off the floor so that your dog does not have to bend over as far to eat. These were created to try to help prevent the serious issue of bloat in some breeds, but studies have shown that elevated feeders can potentially contribute to bloat. Most experts say an elevated feeder is unnecessary and potentially problematic. If you are adopting a dog that has neck or mobility issues, then an elevated dog feeder would be something to discuss with your veterinarian as an option.

Collar, Tags, and Leash – One of the first things you will want to do when you get your new puppy is put on his or her collar with identification tags. These tags can be made instantly at any local pet store, or you can order one from an online retailer. It is best to always have your pet's name, your current address, and your phone number on the tag. This is meant to help a stranger return your dog in the event he ever gets loose. You can even add a little note that says "Please Call My Family," which may encourage someone to call.

Food – Your breeder should send a small amount of food home with your puppy to get you through the first couple of days. It's best to continue with this same brand of food as it is probably high-quality and will save your puppy any intestinal upset from switching. If you do wish to switch foods, talk with your breeder about how to do it safely. They will probably recommend you switch the puppy gradually by mixing in his current food with the new food over a period of a few days.

Puppy-safe Toys – Your puppy will have lots of energy and very sharp teeth. In order to save your couch legs or your shoes, you will want to have at least four or five different dog toys for your puppy to choose from. Because you do not yet know what your puppy will prefer, get at least one plush toy, one rubber toy or bone, one rope, and one ball. Buy toys with different squeaker sounds and textures to see which one your puppy will love the most. You may find that plush toys do not last long before being ripped to shreds, or you may find that your new puppy loves carrying that stuffed elephant all around the house.

Though they may be small, the puppy teeth of a Yorkipoo can still cause serious damage, so don't take them lightly!

Grooming Brush – Yorkipoos have high grooming demands and need to be brushed frequently to prevent matting. As a puppy, your Yorkipoo will not need the brushing his future coat will eventually demand, as his coat will change in texture. But it is a good idea to get him used to the

Photo Courtesy of Kim & Kerry Neck

brush right from the start to avoid any anxiety later. Start with a small, basic medium-bristle brush. Additional information on grooming will be provided in Chapter 12.

Puppy Training Treats – It is essential to have a safe bag of treats to help with potty training and teaching basic commands. Look for soft treats that are healthy and natural. Be sure that they contain no animal by-product, are grain-free, and contain absolutely no artificial flavors, colors, or preservatives.

Preparing an Indoor Space

"Yorkipoos are highly athletic and intelligent. They can easily climb or jump baby gates and if left alone too long will find outlets for their boredom. They are inquisitive and adventurous. If you are leaving your Yokipoo alone you need to have them in a secure area that they can't escape from and that doesn't have anything hazardous they can chew or ingest. That includes corners of dry wall which can be fatal to your fur baby if ingested in large enough quantities."

JENNIFER EMERT
Jen's Tiny Toys

Crate and Pad – Your puppy will need somewhere safe to stay while you are gone or when you cannot keep a close eye on him, such as at night. Invest in a quality crate and pad that will accommodate your Yorkipoo at his full, adult size. Establish it as a safe place early on in the training process. It would be ideal to buy a crate pad that is washable and has minimal stuffing because chances are, it will be chewed on at some point. More specifics on crates and crate training can be found in Chapter 5.

Puppy Gate or Playpen – You will not want your new puppy to have full range of the house right away. Unless your space allows you to keep your puppy contained in a centralized location, you will probably want to purchase a puppy gate or playpen. The idea is to give your young Yorkipoo his own designated "safe space" where he can play without constant supervision.

A gate that blocks a doorway is a good way to keep your puppy from venturing down a hall, up the stairs, or into a room that is off-limits. But a gate still allows the puppy access to furniture and other things, which could potentially become chew things. A playpen allows much more flexibility, as you can move it around wherever inside or outside of the house you will be. A playpen also keeps any furniture from becoming damaged by those razor-sharp puppy teeth.

Preparing an Outdoor Space

Yorkipoos can be energetic and may benefit from an outdoor space to expend some of that energy. It is important to keep any outdoor area you have a dog-friendly zone and make sure it provides plenty of shade and that water is readily available.

Start preparing your outdoor space ahead of time by removing all chemical products from the outdoor area, including the garage. Any weed or pest killer, fertilizers, antifreeze, or other similar products should be placed somewhere the dog cannot reach.

Although you should never leave your Yorkipoo outside unattended for any amount of time, you will still need to be sure the yard is secure. Check all fencing to be sure there are no gaps between the fence and the ground. Make sure all gates latch completely, and there is no way for your dog to

*Photo Courtesy
of Julie Gigliotti*

escape. While the desire to "escape" is not necessarily strong within this crossbreed, they can be known for digging. Your fencing should always be secure, with no gaps at the bottom, so a playful Yorkipoo is not lured away by a noise or a passerby across the street. Always be sure your dog is wearing his collar and tags before allowing him outside for any amount of time.

Yorkipoos are generally good swimmers, but a backyard pool can quickly become a danger without supervision. It is good practice to keep your pool fenced off or somehow separated from your dog so your Yorkipoo does not accidentally get himself into a situation when you are not there to help.

Just like with indoor plants, some outdoor plants and flowers can prove to be poisonous to your dog. Check the list against any plants you may have in your garden and replace those that may be harmful with a safe alternative.

Choosing the Right Veterinarian

It is important to know where you will take your dog for veterinary care before you bring him into your home. Find a vet you trust beforehand so you are prepared from day one to provide him with the best care possible.

When searching for the perfect veterinarian for your new Yorkipoo, you may be tempted to go online and read reviews. Beware that not all reviews are an accurate depiction of an establishment. Instead, start with word of mouth. Ask fellow dog owners which vet they prefer and which ones they would avoid. Make a list of the most favorable and start with those.

Next, eliminate some from your list based on location. In an emergency, you will want to have chosen a vet that is nearby. If there are any clinics on your list that you feel are too far in the event of a crisis, cross them off.

Call all the remaining clinics on your list and inquire about their prices. You can get a good comparison by asking what they charge for a round of shots, a spay or neuter, and an X-ray. Make notes of what each clinic charges and how they accept payment. Do they demand it all upfront or do they offer payment plans? Also make note of the friendliness of the office staff when you call. Did they offer the information willingly or seem put out? You don't want to commit to a vet clinic with unhelpful office staff. That could make any visit an unpleasant experience.

If after all of the above steps you still haven't decided, call each clinic and ask to make an appointment to visit in person. While on your visits, ask the staff or the vet if they have any other Yorkipoos as patients or have experience with the breed. You will likely find that one of the offices is a better fit for you and your puppy than the others and your decision will then be easy. It is important to trust your veterinarian and feel comfortable in their clinic so don't settle on a vet without taking all the necessary steps.

CHAPTER 4
Bringing Home Your Yorkipoo

There is nothing more exciting than the day you get to pick up your new Yorkipoo from the breeder! You've done your research, prepared your home and yard, purchased all the needed supplies, and now all that's left is to bring your puppy home. You may find yourself a bit anxious, wondering how everything will go, but if you follow the tips below, pick-up day should be fun, exciting, and trouble free.

Photo Courtesy of Robyn Cook

Picking Up Your Yorkipoo

When you arrive at the breeding facility at your appointed time, your breeder should have the puppy ready to go in a designated pick-up area. The puppy may be in a pen playing with other puppies that are leaving on the same day. Try not to let the adorable sight of your new Yorkipoo keep you from hearing the important information your breeder will give you!

Before you leave, your breeder should give you detailed information on your puppy's vet records, current shots, future shots, and dewormings. They should remind you of any stipulations of the health guarantee and advise you on a feeding schedule. All of this information as well as breed-specific care tips should be neatly presented in a packet of some sort along with registration papers.

CELEBRITY YORKIPOOS

In the Doghouse

Khloe the Yorkipoo is an incredibly lucky pup. Not only is Khloe owned by American actress Kyle Richards, but as part of the TV show Barkitecture, Khloe and her four furry siblings received a designer doghouse in the style of a colonial home. Complete with black shutters and a landscaped front yard, the doghouse is modeled after Khloe's mom's home in Encino, California, which is also the former home of Smokey Robinson. Tyler Cameron and Delia Kenza are the hosts of the show.

Sometimes a breeder will allow you to take a small blanket or toy home with your dog so that the smell of his litter can comfort him during the transition. It may be beneficial to ask ahead of time if this is an option in order to know if you need to provide the blanket before pick-up day.

The Ride Home

Depending on how far you have to travel to pick up your puppy, you will want to plan accordingly. It is not uncommon for a puppy to get motion sickness and vomit on the ride home, so you might request that the breeder withhold food for that morning. Regardless of how long the trip is, you will want to be sure to take a bowl and a bottle of water for your puppy in the case of an unexpected delay like a flat tire.

There are a couple of options when it comes to transporting your new Yorkipoo. Some people like to take a crate and let the puppy ride home that way. If you do plan to transport the puppy in a crate, place only towels

Photo Courtesy of Bianca Jacques

in the bottom of the crate so that the crate pad is not soiled on the trip. Also, take care to drive smoothly, so you do not jostle your puppy more than necessary.

Not all crates will withstand the force of a crash, and some can even become more dangerous for your dog in the event of a crash. When not properly secured to the vehicle, the crate can become a projectile, injuring your puppy and possibly other passengers in the car. You can visit the Center for Pet Safety (CPS) website for a list of tested and approved travel crates.

If you are thinking of buying a harness for your dog to use in the car, know that they are not all created equally. The Center for Pet Safety performed a Harness Crashworthiness Study in 2013, and results showed that only one of eleven brands tested performed at the level advertised. Some were even deemed "catastrophic failures." Do diligent research on each brand before making your decision, so you can be sure you get a safe one.

Don't be tempted to let the puppy ride in your lap. This is very dangerous for your dog. In the event of a crash, the puppy can be killed by the airbag or become a projectile. Even braking too hard can cause injury to an unsecured puppy.

Before beginning the journey home, allow your puppy to use the restroom on a patch of grass. Praise him if he does, and then begin your trip home. The ride home should be a positive experience for all and can be a great bonding opportunity for you and your puppy. Enjoy those first moments together as a new family!

The First Night

"Your new Yorkipoo puppy will cry the first few nights. If you let them snuggle next to you, it will calm them and they'll be happy, but they will also expect to be allowed to do it from then on, so only do the first few nights what you're willing to do long term!"

LINDA OSBORNE
Pocket Puppies

For the first night home, you will want to have already designated a special place for your puppy to sleep. Many people choose to put the puppy's crate in their room, but you could also put it in a separate room, as long as you can hear the puppy when he needs to go outside to relieve himself. Try to pick a designated area and leave it so that you and your new Yorkipoo can quickly get into a routine.

Before bed, take your puppy outside and wait for ten to fifteen minutes for him to relieve himself. If the puppy does not, wait ten minutes, and then try again. Repeat this process for however long it takes your puppy to go and then put him directly into the crate for bed with his special blanket or toy from the breeder. It may be helpful for nighttime potty runs if you keep the crate by your bed.

The first night home can be daunting and scary for both you and your puppy. That crate can look lonely and uncomfortable for your new Yorkipoo. There will probably be a lot of whining and crying for the first few nights. After all, this will be the very first time your puppy has spent the night away from his mom and siblings. Although it will be tempting to pull your puppy out of the crate and let him sleep with you, it would be best for everyone if you resist the urge and allow your puppy to self-soothe in the crate.

Remember that your puppy will probably need to be taken outside to relieve himself several times a night. When your puppy wakes you in the night, it is best to take him outside, then immediately return him to the crate to sleep. This will teach him that nighttime is for sleeping and not for playing.

If your puppy is having a difficult time sleeping in the crate or keeps you awake with his crying, try talking to your puppy or rubbing his head through the crate to help calm him. The most important thing you can do in the first few days is to make your puppy feel loved and secure. Bonds you form with each other in the early days will last throughout your dog's lifetime, and they will make all aspects of dog ownership that much more enjoyable.

Photo Courtesy of Tammy Bentley

Photo Courtesy of Jennifer Nelson

After a few nights, the bedtime whining should stop, and your puppy should come to find his crate a cozy place to sleep. As you and your Yorkipoo puppy adjust to life with each other, routines will form, and things will get much easier.

The First Vet Visit

Some breeders stipulate that you must take your puppy to the vet within a few days for a checkup. If this is the case, you will want to call and make an appointment with your chosen vet before you pick up your puppy. Be sure to take all records given to you by the breeder for the vet to include in your Yorkipoo's file.

The first appointment will typically be a general checkup to make sure your puppy is in good health. Your puppy will be weighed, and the vet will examine eyes, ears, nose, heart, and lungs. They will look at your dog's skin and coat condition and examine the teeth and mouth. They may take a stool sample to check for parasites. If it is time for your puppy's next round of shots, they will get them at this appointment.

The first vet appointment should be relatively quick and easy. Take this opportunity to ask your vet any questions you may have about feeding or

Photo Courtesy of Karri Meyers

caring for your new puppy. If you have made a list of questions, do not be afraid to pull it out, and make sure you get thorough answers.

Your first days with your new puppy will probably be a combination of wonderful and frustrating. You may get a little less sleep than normal, but the bond you and your puppy are creating during the early days will be well worth the work you are putting in now, no matter how many accidents you have to clean up along the way.

The Cost of Ownership

Many dog owners underestimate how expensive it is to own and properly care for a dog, often taking only the initial purchase price into consideration. While this is definitely a factor, there are a number of other expenses that need to be considered as well. Your Yorkipoo is completely dependent on you for everything, and it's important to be prepared for all of the responsibilities and financial requirements that come with owning one.

The Yorkipoo is what some would call a "Designer Dog," and people will pay significant amounts of money to acquire one despite the breed not being recognized by the American Kennel Club. Depending on location, Yorkipoo puppies will sell anywhere from $1,000 to $4,000.

Purchase price is not the only cost to consider. The first year of a dog's life can be expensive. When you consider the supplies you will need to buy, veterinary visits, and training classes, the cost can really add up. Most puppies come with their first round of shots but you will need to be sure they get the rest from a vet. It is also important to remember, unless you plan to breed your Yorkipoo, that the cost of a spay or neuter can vary depending on location but generally costs from $75 to $250 or more.

Because Yorkipoos are very small dogs, they cost on average $200 to $400 to feed a year, depending on the food. The premium dog food brands may seem expensive, but they will ultimately lead to better health and overall quality of life.

Vet bills are typically the biggest expense for dog owners. Depending on where you live, the office fee is about $50, and an exam can be upwards of $100. A spay or neuter operation can cost up to $200. Vaccines are relatively cheap at between $20 and $30 each, but testing for anything from heartworm to diagnostic bloodwork can cost anywhere from $20 to $250. If there is a more serious illness or injury, things can get incredibly expensive in a hurry. X-rays and ultrasounds can cost $300 to $400. Anesthesia and surgery procedures for emergencies can run into thousands of dollars.

Pet insurance can help to offset some of these costs, but it can cost an average of $500-$600 per year.

Also, consider the cost of boarding your Yorkipoo when you are away for an extended period. If you travel often and do not plan to take your dog, these costs can add up quickly. Look into local boarding facilities to find pricing for your area.

There can also be costs associated with living with your dog. Leasing agents and landlords usually require a pet deposit when you sign your lease, and these usually run between $200 and $700.

Grooming is another expense that needs to be considered. A bath is relatively inexpensive at $20-$40, but anything more than that can be quite costly. A full grooming experience, which your Yorkipoo will need often, can be as much as $120.

Training can also be an unexpected cost. If you opt to seek assistance from a professional, an hour with a private in-home trainer will cost around $100 per session, while a 6-week group class costs an average of $200-$300.

While many of the above costs are optional, it is still wise to consider all of the potential costs of owning and raising your Yorkipoo before you bring him home. The Yorkipoo is not a dog suitable for everyone. The cost of the dog alone can be high. However, if you are financially able to purchase and care for a Yorkipoo, he will reward you with a lifetime of spunk, loyalty, love, and companionship.

CHAPTER 5
Being a Puppy Parent

Whether you have raised a puppy or you are a first-time puppy parent, you will undoubtedly encounter new things. Every dog is different and comes with its own joys and troubles. This chapter will review many of the potential challenges you will encounter with your growing Yorkipoo and help you navigate through them as smoothly as possible.

Photo Courtesy of Denise Murphy

Have Realistic Expectations

The first thing you should remember before becoming a puppy parent is that it's not always fun. Having a puppy is hard work and takes a lot of time and dedication. Caring for a puppy involves getting up in the middle of the night to take your dog outside, going through an entire bottle of stain remover cleaning up accidents, and always keeping a watchful eye to be sure nothing is being destroyed by those sharp puppy teeth. No matter how well-mannered your particular puppy may seem, almost no puppy parents get by completely unscathed, and many lose a pair or two of shoes along the way.

CELEBRITY YORKIPOOS

Bubba

★★★★★

Bubba is a six-pound F1B Yorkipoo from Seattle with over five thousand followers on Instagram (@bubbatheyorkiepoo). An F1B Yorkipoo is either 25 percent poodle and 75 percent Yorkie, or 25 percent Yorkie and 75 percent poodle. These hybrids are achieved by breeding an F1 Yorkipoo with a purebred dog of one of the two breeds which make up the genetic hybrid, in this case, a poodle or Yorkshire Terrier.

If you think raising your Yorkipoo will be easy, reconsider. Puppies are challenging. However, the reward you will receive after going through the challenging phases together will be a well-mannered, properly trained, loyal, and loving companion that will always stick by your side.

Chewing

One of the most frustrating things about caring for a puppy is the chewing. Chewing is a way for puppies to explore the world and also to relieve any pain caused by incoming adult teeth. It is inevitable and unstoppable, so don't reprimand your puppy for doing what comes naturally. Instead, be sure he has plenty of safe toys or rubber bones to chew. That way, your puppy will not be tempted by the leg of the coffee table.

If you catch your puppy chewing on something inappropriate, remove the item or the puppy from the situation and give him an appropriate chew toy. This positive "take and replace" technique is much more effective than yelling at or punishing the puppy. Never let your puppy chew on your fingers or hands. This is a habit that is very difficult to break once established.

If your puppy is a persistent chewer, you may want to invest in some bitter-apple spray. This is intended to deter dogs from chewing due to its bad taste.

Chewing due to teething will most likely stop when all your puppy's adult teeth have come in, around five to six months of age. However, some dogs chew more than others and will continue the habit into young adulthood. In these cases, it is important to always have a safe and desirable chew toy available for your dog.

Photo Courtesy
of Bianca Jacques

Digging

Dogs dig for many reasons. Some dogs dig out of boredom, some because they're hot and want to lie in the cool dirt, and some just for the fun and adventure of it. Despite their cute and dainty stature, Yorkipoos can be avid diggers—they get it from their Yorkshire Terrier roots! If you find yourself with a spunky Yorkipoo that loves to get his paws into the dirt, grass, or gravel, you may need to take some precautions around the yard to keep your plants, lawn, and dog safe.

If your Yorkipoo is trying to dig under a fence, try to determine the reason he may be doing this. Is he not getting enough mental stimulation? The curiosity and energetic nature of a bored Yorkipoo could lead him to seek out an adventure under the fence if the opportunity presents itself. Read more about Yorkipoos and safe fencing in Chapter 3.

If digging gets out of control, you may need to take a different approach. Try letting your dog outside under supervised conditions only. Allow your dog to do his business and then offer him a game of fetch. If you allow your digging Yorkipoo to entertain himself, you may find little craters in your yard.

Barking and Growling

Barking is a favorite pastime for the Yorkipoo so be prepared to hear it often. The Yorkipoo makes a great watch dog and will sound the alarm for almost anything he sees. This is a normal characteristic of this breed and is not necessarily a problem.

A well-bred Yorkipoo may be wary of strangers but should not be aggressive by nature. If you're in the middle of a tug-of-war match with your new puppy, and you hear him let out a vicious growl, the puppy is usually not growling out of aggression. When puppies play, they will often display loud barking, growling, chasing, and pouncing. This is natural in a puppy's development and is how he would be playing with his littermates to establish new skills and better coordination.

If you want to discourage play fighting, don't do it by punishing your puppy. These are natural behaviors that should simply be ignored. If your puppy begins to play too rough and bark and growl, stop playing immediately and walk away. Come back when the puppy settles down. If your puppy continues to play too rough, repeat the process until your puppy grasps the idea of what is and is not acceptable. This will take time but is well worth the effort.

If your dog seems truly agitated or begins nipping and biting in a way that seems defensive, it may be time to schedule a trip to see the vet. Truly agitated growling and biting behavior in a previously well-mannered dog can indicate a health problem that may be causing your dog pain.

Separation Anxiety

"There is an adjustment period with any new puppy that will last their first couple weeks they are away from their mother, and litter-mates. Be patient! Be sure they are eating & drinking as they should be, and do not over-stress them during this time. Playing with your new puppy is wonderful - over exhausting the puppy is not."

MARY LISA CARTER
Sunny Day Puppies

Most puppies will whine or bark when left alone. This is normal behavior and will typically stop as the dog becomes accustomed to short spans of time alone. However, a dog with separation anxiety will bark and pace persistently until you return. He may become destructive, chewing and clawing things out of distress. Even a housetrained dog may urinate or defecate in the house repeatedly when left alone if he suffers from separation anxiety. In extreme cases, a dog may display signs of coprophagia, a condition when a dog defecates and then consumes his stool.

The cause of separation anxiety is unknown and can occur in any dog. Because Yorkipoos need a lot of attention and companionship, they are highly likely to display separation anxiety when left alone. Treating separation anxiety takes patience and understanding. Dogs are pack animals and instinctually do not like to be alone. The anxiety they feel stems from a primal fear of being abandoned.

It may be helpful to take your dog for a walk or play fetch with him for a while just before you leave the house. Hopefully, this will tire your dog out, and he will be too exhausted to get worked up while you're gone. You can also try leaving your Yorkipoo with an interactive toy. Try a treat ball or a dog puzzle that will reward him with treats periodically. This may be just enough distraction to get your dog through his time alone. Make this toy or puzzle a special thing your dog only gets when he's alone. This can help positively reinforce that being alone can be a treat.

If the separation anxiety is severe and nothing seems to work, make an appointment with your vet to check that there is nothing else going on. They may be able to advise you on some safe ways to keep your dog calm when you have to leave the house without him.

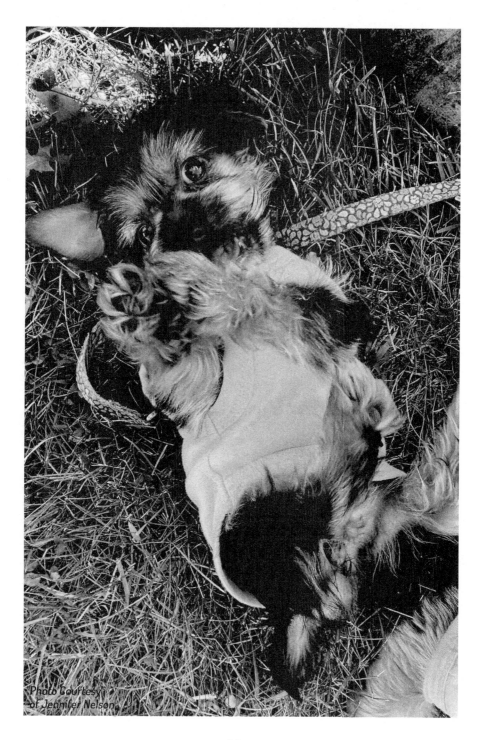

Photo Courtesy
of Jennifer Nelson.

Crate Training Basics

Dogs are not true den animals by nature, but they need a safe, quiet space to go to when they feel scared or anxious. In the wild, dogs and wolves only den when they rear puppies. These dens are usually holes dug in the ground by the mother wolf. The holes are abandoned when the puppies are old enough to travel with the pack. Although domesticated dogs' ancestors didn't spend their days in a den, that doesn't mean your new puppy won't find comfort in a "den" of his own in your house.

Crate training is a controversial topic among dog owners. Some believe the crate is a cage and inhumane. Others believe the crate is a necessary tool

Photo Courtesy
of Nora Larkins

used to protect and secure a dog. The fact is, crate training your Yorkipoo makes puppy ownership more convenient for you and safer for your puppy. When done properly, crating your dog is an excellent tool for housetraining and will set your dog up for success from the start.

When shopping for a crate, there are multiple types to choose from. These include plastic crates, wire crates, soft crates, and heavy-duty crates. The two main types are plastic and wire. If you plan to travel with your dog by plane, you will need to purchase a plastic crate as these are the only crates allowed for air travel.

Wire crates allow more visibility and airflow. They also fold flat for easy storage when not in use. These crates, depending on the size, often come with a removable divider. You can line your crate with a commercial pad or an old towel or blanket for comfort. Regardless of what type of crate you buy, be sure you get one big enough for your Yorkipoo when he is fully grown, or else you may end up having to buy another one. This shouldn't be an issue for a dog as small as the Yorkipoo. Many crates come with dividers you can use to make the usable area of the crate smaller while your dog is young, and gradually expand as your dog grows.

The key to crate training is positive reinforcement. The crate is intended to be a safe place for your dog, a place he can go for rest and comfort. Do not ever put your dog in the crate as a form of punishment. This sends the message that the crate is a bad place and will create issues going forward. You don't want your dog to view the crate as a "timeout" box, or he will never retreat there willingly.

The first time you introduce your new puppy to the crate, you'll want to have some training treats on hand. Secure the door of the crate to the side so it doesn't accidentally swing closed and scare your puppy. Begin by placing a treat or two outside, near the door of the crate. Depending on how your dog reacts to the crate, slowly place the treats closer until you can put one inside. Your puppy should voluntarily go inside the crate to get the treat.

Don't shut the door of the crate the first few times the puppy goes in. Instead, praise him and allow him to come in and out of the crate freely. After your puppy becomes comfortable with the open crate, guide him inside and gently latch the door. Give him treats from outside the crate and verbally praise him. Only leave him in there for a few moments at first and stay with him. This will help him feel comfortable. Practice this exercise the first day you get your puppy home to get him comfortable with the crate before his first night in it.

Any time you need to crate your dog, make sure to reward him with treats and a special toy. Praise him and make it a fun experience to get inside the crate. Don't leave your dog in the crate for long the first few times, with the exception of nighttime, or he may begin to get anxious and associate those feelings with the crate. Practice leaving your puppy in the crate while you're home for short increments of time, thirty minutes to an hour. Always immediately take your dog outside to his potty area when you let him out of the crate.

It is not reasonable for you to put your dog in a crate without first allowing him to expend his energy. Be sure to exercise your dog thoroughly before expecting him to have any crate time. Doing this will allow him to rest and sleep in his crate while you're away, further minimizing the chances of separation anxiety.

The crate is a tool that should be used responsibly. Never leave your dog in a crate for an extended period or treat the crate like a dog-sitter. Hopefully, with proper training, your puppy will outgrow his need for the crate and will no longer need to be confined to it while you're sleeping or away. If your puppy doesn't view the crate as a place of rest and comfort, you may need to reevaluate the way you're using it.

Photo Courtesy of T. Torres

Leaving Your Dog Home Alone

The first time you leave your Yorkipoo home alone can be nerve-wrack-ing for both of you. Hopefully, you have already introduced your dog to the crate and allowed him to practice spending time alone in it. Before leaving your dog for the first time, play with your dog vigorously to wear him out or take him on a jog or a long walk. When it's time for him to go into the crate, follow the same guidelines outlined in the previous section. Reward your dog with a treat for entering the crate and give him a special "crate only" toy as an additional reward and boredom buster. Interactive treat toys like Kongs work great for this.

When you return from your first trip away, it may seem fitting to greet your puppy excitedly but refrain so you don't make your dog think getting out of the crate is more exciting than going in. Going in the crate should be fun and exciting but getting out should be no big deal. Open the door to the crate casually and without much fuss. Remember, the crate is a safe place of rest for your dog, not a place of punishment or a place of waiting. If you let your dog out of the crate with too much excitement, you will inadvertently train him to be overexcited when the crate door opens.

Crate training takes time and effort. Some dogs take to it quickly and eas-ily, while others need more time and practice. Your Yorkipoo naturally does not like to be left alone, so it is especially important that you don't overuse the crate with a Yorkipoo, causing him anxiety and loneliness. This can lead to social and behavior issues. If you intend to leave your dog home for an extended time while you work, look into dog day care.

CHAPTER 6
Potty Training Your Yorkipoo

"Consistency and 'Praise Parties' are the key to house-training. Give them regular trips to their potty area: 30 minutes after eating and every two hours throughout the day. Use the same command every time 'Go Potty' and then...this is the key...when they go potty where you want them to have an all out Praise Party! Tell them what a good puppy they are and shower them with petting and affection. These little ones are super smart and really want to please you so Praise Parties will get your fur baby on the right track very quickly."

JENNIFER EMERT
Jen's Tiny Toys

Photo Courtesy of Nora Larkins

Methods of Potty Training

Potty training your puppy will take a lot of time and energy. It typically takes four to six months for a dog to be fully potty trained, sometimes longer. The only proper way to potty train is by using positive reinforcement. Gone are the days when people told you to reprimand a dog and "rub his nose in it." This method simply does not work and is a cruel punishment for a puppy that doesn't know any better.

The goal is to teach your new puppy that your home is also his. Instinctually, dogs will not soil the places where they eat and sleep. Slowly introduce your dog to small, controlled areas of your house until he views the space as his own. This could be in a puppy playpen or a wire crate in the room with you when you first start the training. Over time, you can expand the area your dog is allowed in until, eventually, he knows that he should only relieve himself outside.

CELEBRITY YORKIPOOS

Graziela Gems

Graziela Kaufman, owner and designer for the company Graziela Gems, is the proud owner of a Yorkipoo. Graziela Gems is a high-end jewelry company admired by celebrities such as Taylor Swift, Jennifer Lawrence, and Jennifer Lopez. Graziela also owns a rescued Bernese Mountain Dog and two cats. She's a self-described animal lover and admits to taking both her dogs and cats for long walks on the beach near her home.

Take your puppy out often, about every hour, and reward him freely with verbal praise and treats. Try to consistently take him to the same area so he will smell his scent and know that it's time to potty. Make this time with your puppy calm and all about business. Do your best to ignore his attempts to play until after he's finished so that he doesn't forget the reason he went outside in the first place.

It may take ten to fifteen minutes, but when your dog relieves himself, celebrate enthusiastically and reward him with a treat. This will help show him that going potty outside is a positive and fun experience. Your Yorkipoo will want to please you, so once he gets the notion that this is what makes you happy, he will be much easier to train.

Photo Courtesy
of Lisa Butler

Using the Crate for Potty Training

The crate is a great tool to use for potty training because it allows you to control your puppy in a small space during the times you can't supervise him. If you're using a wire crate, make sure the area is big enough for your dog to comfortably stand and turn around in but not big enough that he can take several steps from side to side. This will prevent him from soiling one side and sleeping on the other.

If you're not sure how often you should take your dog outside, a good rule of thumb to follow for a young puppy is for every month old he is, that's how many hours he can wait to go potty. That doesn't mean that you should only take your puppy out that often, because if you do, you will most likely be cleaning up a lot of accidents. This is simply a guideline for how long a young puppy can be left in the crate before needing to go out. Never leave your puppy or dog in the crate longer than four to six hours except at night, when you should only take him out as he wakes.

When you wake up in the morning, immediately take your dog outside to the designated potty area. If you're planning to put your dog back into the crate while you're gone for work, take the time to exercise him thoroughly before you do. This will help your dog rest better while you're gone. You will need to come home to let your dog out at lunchtime. Follow the same procedure before putting him back into the crate.

If you can't get back home to take your dog out at lunch, you will need to make other arrangements. Doggy daycare is a great option. It will help you continue the potty-training process and also help with socialization. Usually, these places require certain vaccinations, so be sure to call and check ahead of time. If doggy daycare is not an option, call a friend or family member to come by and let your puppy out for you. You can even hire a dog walker to come and exercise your pup while you are away. Go through a reputable service like Care.com so you can read references and know they've had a background check.

If you absolutely have to leave your dog in the crate or a puppy-proofed room for longer than you should, you can use a puppy pad on one side of the crate. This will slow down the training process because you will, at some point, have to remove the pads and retrain your dog that the only acceptable place to go is outside. Remember, Yorkipoos are not happy alone and will become anxious. If you are planning to leave your dog home every day while you are at work, you should consider a different breed.

The First Few Weeks

The first few weeks of potty training your Yorkipoo will be challenging. In the beginning, take your dog out every hour or so during daytime hours. He may not need to go every time but give him ten to fifteen minutes to try. Even if you have a fenced backyard, it will benefit you to take your dog outside on a leash. This will allow you to control where he goes and help him not be too distracted. Don't forget to praise him verbally and with a treat as soon as he finishes. This is an important step in helping him realize this is what you want him to do.

*Photo Courtesy
of Karri Meyers*

How to Handle Accidents

Accidents are going to happen, so go ahead and buy that odor-neutralizing cleaner! Learning to potty outside is tough for a young puppy and requires patience by all. If you have been trying to train your dog to go on the grass, accidents on rugs and carpets are inevitable. The feeling of the carpet on a dog's paws is very similar to the feeling of grass and can sometimes trick a young puppy into thinking he can relieve himself there. If this becomes a problem, you might want to temporarily remove any rugs from your puppy's designated area until he gets the hang of going outside.

If you catch your dog in the act, quickly pick him up and take him outside to the potty area. Don't punish or yell at your dog. Most often, accidents are a direct result of the owner not taking the dog out enough. Sometimes a dog will soil a carpet just minutes after coming inside. Regardless, your puppy is still learning and should not be punished for the mistake. Punishing will only confuse your dog and prolong the potty-training process.

Pros and Cons of Doggy Doors

Doggy doors can be beneficial in your efforts to potty train, especially for older dogs. If you have a secured backyard, a doggy door can allow your dog to let himself out as he pleases. This could mean fewer accidents and a shorter training period. You should never let your dog go outside unsupervised unless you know the backyard is completely secure, and your dog can't escape. Adding a doggy door is not for everyone, though, and you should review this list of pros and cons before making your decision.

Installation: Installing a doggy door is making a permanent change to your home, and they are notoriously difficult to install. If you don't own your home, a doggy door is probably not an option for you.

Unwanted Visitors: Doggy doors are great for allowing your dog to freely come in and out of your home, but they may unintentionally offer that same freedom to unwanted wild animals as well. Nobody wants a tiny masked bandit coming in under the cover of night! However, this could be solved by getting a doggy door that stays locked until it senses a microchip in your dog's collar as he approaches.

Indoor Cats: If you have an indoor cat, it will be nearly impossible to keep him from leaving through an unlocked doggy door. If your cat has been declawed, this is particularly dangerous because your cat will have no defense from predators. If you have an indoor cat who already loves to go outside, a doggy door will allow him to bring his "treasures" inside the house.

Photo Courtesy of Lori Duchak

Finding a dead snake or bird in the house is probably not what the doggy door was meant for.

Securing the Yard: Before allowing your dog unsupervised time in the yard, you must be sure it's a safe area. Be sure the fence is secure and add a lock to any gate so neighborhood kids or thieves cannot let your dog out. If your dog is a digger, then you may have a problem with him digging out to go explore. This is dangerous because he may encounter cars on his big adventure outside the yard.

Backyard Pool: Another danger to consider in the backyard is a pool. Even if your dog enjoys swimming, he should never be allowed near the pool unless you are out there with him. Swimming alone is dangerous, even for a dog. Allowing full access to the house and pool also permits your dog to come in and out freely while sopping wet, causing a big mess for you to clean up when you get home.

Fire Escape: One positive to a doggy door is it allows your dog to escape the house in case of an emergency. This could potentially save your dog's life in the event of a fire.

If you know your yard is safe and secure and you want to install a doggy door to aid in training, go ahead! You will still need to confine your dog's indoor privileges to a small space while still allowing access to the doggy door. This can be done by using a playpen set up against the wall.

A doggy door is not always a good option, but in the right scenario, it can be very helpful. For elderly or disabled owners who have a more difficult time getting around, a doggy door allows the dog to relieve himself in the proper area without any burden to the owner.

If you decide on a doggy door, be prepared for a little bit of training; your puppy will not know how to use it otherwise. The first time you teach him to use it, give him a gentle push through and have another person on the other side, ready with a small treat and plenty of praise. Do this several times, in both directions. Once your puppy allows you to push him through without resistance, go to the opposite side of the doggy door, extend your hand through to the puppy, and allow him to smell the treat in your hand. Use the treat to lure him through. Finally, call him from the other side, and give a treat when he goes through by himself. If you spend 5 or 10 minutes a day doing this, your Yorkipoo should be going through the door by himself within a week.

CHAPTER 7
Socializing Your Yorkipoo

"As soon as your puppy is fully immunized, start having play dates with your puppy and other puppies or dogs. Be sure the other puppies or dogs are either within the same weight range as your puppy or are very mindful about how they behave around your puppy. 'Praise Parties' work here too. Let your fur baby know when you are proud of them."

JENNIFER EMERT
Jen's Tiny Toys

Importance of Socialization

Yorkipoos are friendly to their companions but can sometimes be unsure of people they do not know. They will typically warm up quickly and greet other people and dogs with a friendly tail wag. However, without proper socialization, your dog may not fully come into his friendly potential. By beginning your dog's socialization early, you can be sure that he will be able to coexist with any people or dogs he encounters in any environment. This will make life easier for you if you take your dog to the park, restaurants, or other crowded outdoor events.

Photo Courtesy
of Tj Torres

Behavior Around Other Dogs

Imagine a world where people greeted each other the way dogs do by sniffing, circling, and jumping up and down playfully. That would be quite a silly sight! Luckily for us, we humans have strict social guidelines to follow when we encounter each other. Dogs also have a set of social rules, but they are not nearly as strict as ours.

YORKIPOOS IN BOOKS
Doggies in Sweaters

Doggies Don't Wear Sweaters, by Shirley L. Larke, is an illustrated book for children that the author hopes will inspire a love of reading in young people. The book follows the author's dog, a silver-gray Yorkipoo named Brooklyn Mashelle Larke, who thinks that she's a person!

Much like people, dogs greet each other differently at a first meeting than they greet an old friend, and much of it depends on the individual dog's personality. Dogs typically greet each other in one or all of the following ways:

Sniffing: Probably the most notable canine ritual is the sniff test. When dogs greet one another, they may begin with the muzzle or go straight for the backside. Sometimes the sniff will be brief, and sometimes it can seem like a full-blown investigation. Unless one dog seems uncomfortable, this is perfectly normal behavior and doesn't need to be stopped. Once the dogs have satisfied their sniffers, they can move on to the next step in the canine greeting.

Play Stance: Have you ever seen a dog approach another dog and immediately go into a play bow? This behavior is simply one dog attempting to initiate play with another. It's like he's saying, "Hey there! Do you want to be friends and play together?" Even a quick, playful growl accompanied by a friendly tail wag is acceptable. Again, as long as neither dog seems stressed, there is no need to stop this behavior. Even if the other dog declines the offer to play, that doesn't mean the meeting was not successful.

Exerting Dominance: This particular greeting is probably the least endearing but is still acceptable in the canine world. One dog may exert his dominance by being the first to sniff and by non-aggressively showing the other dog he is in charge. This could include mounting. This process may be obvious to you, or it may all happen so quickly that you don't even notice until little Sparky rolls over to show his belly in submission. As with the other behaviors, these are the natural social ways of dogs and should not be stopped unless there is real aggression or stress. Dogs take social cues well and are pretty good at keeping each other in line. If one dog is displeased, he will probably let the other know quickly.

Small Dog Syndrome

Small dog syndrome develops when a small dog is allowed to engage in behaviors that a larger dog would not. This may include excessive barking at people, lunging at other animals or people, snarling, snapping, and other dominance behaviors.

Oftentimes, dogs of small stature, including Yorkipoos, will try to make up for their lack of size by exhibiting these behaviors. Because they are not as invasive or "dangerous" as a larger dog, they are frequently allowed to continue with these bad habits.

Instead of accepting this as a reality of small dogs, take action through training to stop the behaviors when they begin so you are not dealing with the issue for years to come.

Photo Courtesy
of Lori Duchak

Safe Ways to Socialize with Other Pets

The way dogs behave around each other can vary from breed to breed and dog to dog. If you're bringing your Yorkipoo home as a puppy, socializing him with other dogs should be easy. In general, puppies are more adaptable and willing to meet other dogs. Socialization should begin as early as possible, but be sure not to allow your puppy to have close contact with dogs you don't know until he has had his complete series of puppy shots.

If you choose to socialize your puppy with a leash on, keep your puppy close on a leash or on the other side of a barrier, such as a gate when you make introductions with other dogs, especially those that are older or larger. Preferably all other dogs should also be leashed or somehow restrained in case anything goes wrong.

Allow the dogs to greet each other for a few seconds and then walk away. Each owner should distract their dog at this point until they are no longer interested in the other dog. If the initial interaction went well, allow the dogs to come together again in the same manner. Keep the leash loose so the dog can maneuver but not so loose it becomes a tangled mess. Read each dog's body language to determine how the greeting is going. Bodies should be relaxed, and there should be no staring contests. As the dogs become comfortable and relaxed with each other, you will be able to let them off-leash, and they can have supervised play.

Some trainers believe first-time dog greetings should always be done off-leash so that the dogs behave and greet each other more naturally. They believe that some dogs will feel trapped by the leash and become more defensive in nature, making the greeting unnatural and awkward. If this is the method you choose, make sure the owners of both dogs are fully compliant and willing to meet in a safe and neutral fenced area.

A first-time greeting should never be done in one of the dogs' yards. This could be seen as an invasion of territory for some dogs and cause a defensive reaction. Allow the dogs to meet but monitor their body language. If they use the body language described above, you don't need to interfere. But if either dog seems stiff, uncomfortable, or agitated, separate the dogs and use distractions to get their attention off of each other. Off-leash greetings can bring a greater risk if you don't know the other dog well and should only be done with friendly, pre-socialized dogs. Safety is the most important thing when socializing your dog, so only do what you feel comfortable with.

Socializing Adult Dogs

If you're bringing an adult Yorkipoo into your home, the socialization process may take some extra time and careful planning. Depending on the dog's previous situation, he may not be used to other dogs. Often with a rescue, you don't know exactly what his life has held up until the point he was rescued. He may have been kept in a cage his whole life, abused by his owner, or even previously attacked by a dog. All of these things are unknowns that could have a significant impact on his social abilities.

Be patient with your dog, no matter his age, and allow him to socialize on his terms. If your dog seems to have trouble socializing, take it slow and avoid putting your dog in situations that will cause him stress. This will only cause setbacks.

When dealing with an unsocialized adult dog, begin slowly at home. Take your dog on a walk around your neighborhood where he can see other dogs indirectly. He should eventually become comfortable enough to walk by other dogs in their backyards or on leashes without becoming stressed. When he has successfully mastered these indirect encounters, it's time to move on to the next step.

If you have a neighbor with a dog, this is a great place to start direct socialization. These dogs will probably encounter each other at one point or another and will benefit by getting to know each other. Ask your neighbor and arrange a time to allow both dogs to meet, on leashes, in a neutral part of the yard. Take things slow and give them space if either seems stressed. Follow the three-second rule and then walk away and distract each dog. Allow the dogs to come together again if the first encounter went well. If it doesn't seem to be going well, that's okay! Allow the dogs to just be in the yard at the same time until they become used to each other, and then gradually allow them to interact more as it seems appropriate.

Keep your demeanor calm and stress-free so that your dog doesn't pick up on any tension. It's all about establishing trust between you and your dog and between your dog and your neighbor's dog. Speak to your neighbor and his dog in a friendly and confident tone to help show your Yorkipoo that the visitors are not a threat. With enough positive interactions, your dog should eventually warm up to them and become more social.

If you don't have a neighboring dog, call a friend with a dog, or take your dog to a dog park. A dog park can be overwhelming, depending on how many dogs are there. So, this may be a last resort as a place to socialize. Begin by just walking around the perimeter at a comfortable distance. Listen to your dog and take his cues. If he seems comfortable, allow him to interact more closely with a dog through the fence. If he remains calm, praise him.

Reward him for positive encounters and remove him from negative ones. Try to only let him interact with dogs that are also calm. It will not help the situation to engage with a loud, barking, rambunctious dog through the fence. This could cause stress for an unsocialized dog and stop progress.

Another great option for socializing your Yorkipoo with other dogs is to enroll in a beginning obedience class at a local training center. Call your local pet supply store or ask your breeder for referrals. This should only be done after he has had his full series of puppy shots and is beginning to mature. Arrive at least 10-15 minutes before the class begins and sit quietly with your dog (on his lead) so that he can get accustomed to the environment and begin to feel confident with other dogs. Once the class begins, he will be focused on learning some basics of obedience, while surrounded by other dogs. You will also learn how to teach your Yorkipoo valuable commands, like heel, sit, stay, and come, which will come in very handy throughout his life.

Greeting New People

Introducing a Yorkipoo puppy to new people should be easy. Remember, puppies are generally easy going and take to new friends well. The main thing you will want to teach your puppy about meeting new people is not to jump. This can be challenging because a tiny jumping Yorkipoo may seem cute to some; however, to some it is a source of irritation. It's much harder to correct the behavior if it was once allowed.

Ideally, when approached by a person, your puppy should remain calm and keep all four paws on the ground. If you need to stop a jumping habit, begin by teaching your dog an alternate command. "Sit" is a good command to combat jumping because your dog can't do both at the same time. (Learn more about teaching basic commands in Chapter 10.) When your dog gets overly excited and begins to jump, counter by giving the "sit" command. Reward him for sitting and staying calm. If he can't stay calm and continues to jump, leave the room and ignore your dog for thirty seconds to one minute. Return and try again. This process works well for meeting new people, getting the leash out for walks, or any other exciting event that gets your dog jumping.

Introducing a rescue dog to new people can be a different story. Not knowing your dog's past means not knowing if he's had any negative human interactions. Begin any new introductions with people much like you would with dogs, slow and controlled. If your rescue Yorkipoo is a bit socially stunted, you'll have to work to gain his trust. Apply those same principles to anyone you want to introduce to your dog.

Photo Courtesy
of Julie Gigliotti

If you're having guests over, ask those people ahead of time to remain calm and not show the dog much attention. This may help ease your dog's mind and keep him calm. If your guests want to rub and love all over your Yorkipoo, even with the best intentions, it could cause him to become over-excited and stressed. Once calm and comfortable, the dog may be trusting enough to allow a belly rub or two, but it should always be on his own terms. Give your guests some training treats to gain his trust. If your dog is particularly shy and nervous, and you don't see much progress being made, try separating him with a baby gate so that he can observe the people but not feel pressured or overwhelmed.

Don't be afraid to take your dog out into other situations where he can meet people. One of the best places for this is your local big-box home improvement store. Most of these stores not only allow dogs, but welcome them warmly. It's hard to make your way from the electrical department to the lumber area without a dozen or so friendly people asking to say hello and pet your adorable dog! Have a few small treats handy and ask people to give one to your puppy – he will quickly learn that meeting people is a good experience.

With enough patience and diligence, almost any dog can become well-socialized. A friendly Yorkipoo should make the process easy, but it's still important to follow the guidelines above for the safety of your own dog and others.

Yorkipoos and Children

Yorkipoos can bond well with older children; however, they often do not pair well with small children. Due to the Yorkipoo's small size, he can easily be injured by energetic and excited children. It is not that a Yorkipoo cannot bond with young children, it is simply a safety and comfort concern for the dog.

While it may be cute to allow your Yorkipoo to sleep with your children, this should not be allowed. Remember, your Yorkipoo will remain small and delicate even when fully mature. Accidentally rolling over on top of your pup while sleeping is dangerous and could even be fatal.

Always teach your children to be gentle and kind, never pulling ears, hair, or tail. Show them by example the proper way to pet and handle your Yorkipoo so that they understand how to safely handle him. No matter how friendly and trustworthy your dog is, never leave a child and dog alone unattended. This is for the safety of both the child and the dog.

CHAPTER 8
Yorkipoos and Your Other Pets

Interspecies Introductions

To introduce your new puppy to a resident cat, begin by keeping the animals separated and place a blanket or toy with the puppy's scent near the cat. Do the same for the puppy in a different area of the house. Let the dog and the cat sniff and become accustomed to the scents before a face to face interaction.

After exchanging scents, allow your pets to interact indirectly. Keep them separated by a gate or the crate, but allow them to view each other. Depending on their reactions, you may feel comfortable enough to let them loose, but be careful—your puppy probably can't do much damage to your cat, but your cat can definitely harm your puppy if he feels threatened. Try introductions with someone gently holding each animal. Let the two sniff and explore but watch carefully for claws. Praise both animals for calm and reasonable reactions. Stop the introduction immediately if there is any fear or aggression shown.

Most likely, your Yorkipoo pup will want to make friends with your cat and play right away. Your cat, on the other hand, probably won't know how

Photo Courtesy of Nora Larkins

to handle all of this playful affection and will need a place to escape. This escape should be off the ground in an area where your dog can't reach.

Introducing an Older Yorkipoo

You will need to take a different approach to introducing an adult Yorkipoo to a resident cat. While an adult Yorkipoo probably still isn't much of a threat to your cat, your cat can cause your dog significant harm. Begin with the scent exchange described above.

After a day of getting accustomed to the other's scent, allow the two animals to meet through a closed door. Depending on personality, either pet may not be very interested in the other, or the animals may be busting down the door to see who is on the other side. Allow each animal to become calm and relaxed before any face to face interactions.

Once the two have become relaxed and calm on both sides of the door, allow the animals to meet with the dog on a loose leash. Allow a brief inter-action before separating them and diverting their attention. If the initial interaction was calm and peaceful, try again. If you decide to let the two interact with your dog off-leash, always ensure your cat can escape to his safe space, designated just for him.

Cats and dogs can live peacefully together and can even form close bonds, but it probably won't happen overnight.

Aggression and Bad Behavior

Yorkipoos don't typically have issues with aggression unless they have been allowed to behave poorly. However, despite a reputable breeder and good genes, improper treatment can ignite aggression in almost any dog. Animal abuse can cause deep-seated issues for your dog, which man-ifests as growling, snapping, or biting at you or other pets. This is especially important to remember if you're bringing home an adult rescue dog with an unknown past.

If your dog does display aggressive behaviors, first take your dog to the vet to be sure there is no underlying condition causing him pain. Once this is ruled out, it's time to evaluate the dog's current situation. Is there anything causing your Yorkipoo unnecessary stress? Is he being left alone too long? Is he being given enough attention and exercise? A Yorkipoo demands an extremely high level of companionship, and his behavior could suffer from not getting it.

If your Yorkipoo is showing aggression toward other dogs, take the proper steps to socialize him. Go slowly and don't progress to direct

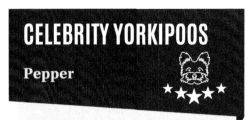

CELEBRITY YORKIPOOS

Pepper

★★★★★

Pepper the Yorkipoo is an Instagram celebrity who has gained a following of over six thousand people with his adorable photos (@pepper_poo). Pepper is frequently joined by his foster friends, both cats and dogs! His hospitality has helped four puppies and thirteen kittens (and counting!) find their forever homes.

interactions until your dog can keep his cool consistently. For dogs dealing with aggression issues, this could take much longer to achieve.

If your dog is showing aggression toward other pets at home, begin by identifying the source. Is it food aggression? Does your dog become possessive over toys or treats? If you identify the source, remove it. If your dog is dealing with food aggression, eliminate the situation by feeding your Yorkipoo in another room, away from all other pets. If he is particularly possessive of a favorite toy, only allow him to have the toy in the confines of his crate or designated alone area. Removing your dog from the stressful situation will not solve the aggression problem, but it will make life easier while you deal with the root cause.

As long as your dog isn't causing any physical harm to you or any other members of your family, continue to work on carefully socializing the dog, rewarding friendly behavior with treats and praise. If the aggression doesn't improve or evolves to physical harm in any way, seek a professional trainer's help immediately. Never leave a potentially aggressive dog alone with another animal or an unfamiliar person.

Rough Play or Aggression?

Many dogs growl and bare their teeth when they play. This does not automatically mean your dog has aggression issues. In fact, sometimes, it can be quite difficult to distinguish between play and aggression.

When your dog and another dog are playfully bowing and taking turns chasing, rolling over, and mouthing each other, these are all signs that they are engaging in play together. Allowing this play to continue offers your dog great practice with social skills and is a wonderful outlet for excess energy.

If the dogs are playing, but one or both seem stiff and tense, there may be more than a playful romp going on between them. Deep, drawn-out growling, staring into the other dog's eyes, and a one-sided chase may all be indications that one or both of the dogs are showing some real aggression, and you may need to end the encounter.

Photo Courtesy
of Christine Schatz

If you're having trouble with your puppy or adult dog playing too rough with you, the best thing to do is ignore him. In a pack of dogs, older dogs will naturally teach the younger pups when enough is enough. They do this by verbal cues and then ending play immediately. Even puppies of the same litter do this to each other. As the owner, you can take the same stance. When play becomes too rough, yip loudly and then walk away, ignoring your dog. After a minute, once the dog seems to have shifted his attention, return to play. Repeat this process until the puppy understands the rough play is not acceptable. Eventually, he will understand the reason you keep walking away and will lessen his intensity.

Be aware of how you approach your dog for play. If you come in swinging and throwing your hands and arms around, this is encouraging your dog to play rough. Use toys instead of your body and keep movements gentle.

What to Do When Pets Don't Get Along

If your Yorkipoo and current pets cannot seem to get along, after using these tips to ease the transition, don't hesitate to call a professional trainer. The sooner you address the issue, the easier it will be to overcome. Allowing your pets to continue coexisting in a stress-filled environment can amplify the problem and could even lead to injury.

CHAPTER 9
Exercising Your Yorkipoo – Physically and Mentally

"Yorkipoos LOVE adventure! Take them with you whenever you can. The mind stimulating toys made for dogs are nice but they tend to figure them out pretty quick so they don't last very long. Outdoor exercise is FUN - walks, stopping & visiting the neighbors, hiking, swimming, digging for mice, these are the things your Yorkipoo will love to do"

MARY LISA CARTER
Sunny Day Puppies

Photo Courtesy
of Jen Berg

Exercise Requirements

All dog breeds need regular exercise to keep them in good shape and your Yorkipoo is no exception. Because of their very small size, Yorkipoos don't need an extremely active lifestyle to thrive. A minimum of a quick walk around the block once a day is all they need to keep them happy and in shape. That said, while he may not be an intense running partner or lap swimming buddy, your Yorkipoo still needs his fair share of activity.

How to Make Exercise Fun

"Your Yorkipoo can be just as happy racing around in a fenced yard as it can be racing around in a large house. The key is to use toys (balls, pull ropes, etc.) to encourage play and running to fetch and bring it back. An hour a day of good physical exercise is key."

JENNIFER EMERT
Jen's Tiny Toys

There are so many ways to make exercising your dog fun and exciting for both of you. Sometimes walking the same block or route in the park can become mundane, but walking your Yorkipoo is not the only way to get your dog's heart pumping. Try some of the following ideas to help you and your dog get past an exercise slump!

Use a Flirt Pole – A flirt pole is basically a stick with a toy attached to the end with a string. It allows you to engage your dog in a game of chase without much movement of your own. You can even use the flirt pole from a seated position. A flirt pole is the perfect solution for owners who are elderly or have limited mobility and cannot run alongside their dog. The flirt pole engages your dog mentally and physically, a win-win!

Play Hide and Seek – Once your dog has mastered basic commands (more on basic commands in Chapter 10) and can sit and stay, try engaging him in a game of hide and seek. Take your dog to a chosen location in the house and have him sit and stay where he is. Your job is to go hide elsewhere in the house and then call him when you are ready.

If your dog won't stay still long enough to allow you to hide, try giving him a treat that will take him half a minute or so to finish. Once he finishes, call to him from your hiding place and see how long it takes him to find you. Keep giving your Yorkipoo encouragement until he figures out where

Photo Courtesy of Lori Kratzer

you are. The game is fun for you and him alike and is a great way to give him exercise on a rainy day!

Play Fetch – There is not much a dog loves more than a game of fetch. Play with a tennis ball, rope, or Frisbee. Mix it up to keep things interesting. Teach your dog to return the item to your lap and this game can be a consistently easy outlet for excess energy.

Scavenger Hunt – A typical dog has up to 300 million olfactory receptors in his nose

FUN FACT
Collegiate Dogs

Study Breaks, an online magazine written and illustrated by college students, voted Yorkipoos as one of the top seven breeds for college students. The magazine cites the Yorkipoo's high energy as a bonus to college students who may become sedentary without proper motivation. The Yorkipoo's size is also a plus, as many college students live in smaller apartments, which makes larger dogs more difficult to house.

and the part of a dog's brain devoted to smell is proportionally 40 times larger than a human's. That means your Yorkipoo has a powerful sniffer! Make mealtime or snack time fun by creating a game out of it and putting that nose to work.

Hide small amounts of food or treats around areas of a room and see if your dog can sniff them out. If you hide them in enough areas, he may find himself running around the room from spot to spot trying to find the sources of the smell. While this may not provide as much exercise as one of the previous suggestions, it is still a way to get a lazy dog motivated on a dreary day.

Dog Day Care – Even if you spend most of your time home with your Yorkipoo, an occasional trip to a local dog day care is a great way to give your pup some play time with other dogs while also allowing you to run errands. After a few hours at day care, your dog will probably be exhausted and ready for a relaxing nap at home.

Importance of Mental Exercise

Although physical exercise usually gets most of the attention, mental stimulation for your Yorkipoo is equally as important. A bored dog is often a destructive dog, especially with an emotionally needy dog like the Yorkipoo.

*Photo Courtesy
of Adele Meighan*

Tips for Keeping Your Yorkipoo Occupied

Many of the suggestions above serve as mental exercise as well as physical. Playing hide and seek, doing scavenger hunts, and using a flirt pole all provide a high amount of direct mental stimulation, as does interacting with other dogs at dog day care.

Another way to mentally stimulate your Yorkipoo is by teaching him a new trick. Learning a new command will help to further build the relationship and trust between you two, resulting in a generally more obedient and willing dog. After he has mastered all of the basic commands, get creative and teach your Yorkipoo some fun tricks like jumping through a hoop, walking backward, or crawling. You can even teach him to retrieve his toys by name and put them back in their designated places.

There are toys and puzzles designed specifically with mental stimulation in mind. Kong makes a range of toys that can keep your dog occupied for a long time and are basically indestructible. A favorite is the "Classic Dog Toy." This is a rubber toy with a hollow center made for stuffing with treats. Kong has a safe line of treats and snacks or you can simply fill the toy with peanut butter. The Kong is dishwasher safe and costs between $8 and $25, depending on size, making it a great, affordable option.

Another option is a dog puzzle. The Trixie Poker Box has four compartments all covered by a lid. Your dog must figure out how each lid can be removed to get the reward waiting inside. All four lids open differently so this will take some real focus and determination on your dog's part. Once your dog figures out the trick to opening all boxes, this puzzle may not present a challenge anymore and he may want to move onto something else, so keep the toy in your arsenal for when your dog must be left alone.

If you prefer a mentally stimulating toy without the use of treats, try getting your Yorkipoo an Outward Hound Hide A Squirrel Puzzle Dog Toy. It's a hollow, plush tree stump with holes around it. Inside there are three plush squirrels that squeak. Your dog will have tons of fun trying to pull the squirrels from the stump. This is a great option for a dog who may need to watch his weight but probably isn't a good idea for a vigorous chewer as the squirrels are plush and can be torn apart with enough effort.

There are also electronic devices that you can control from a mobile device. Clever Pet is a unique system that challenges your dog with sequences, memory games, and electronically released treats or food when solved. This system comes with a light-up pad that shows different colors and patterns. Clever Pet is designed to progressively get more challenging as your dog figures it out. Use the mobile application to track progress and monitor use. This system is wonderful for dogs who are left alone for long

Photo Courtesy
of Ella Leeco

periods. It comes with a $250 price tag but is worth it if it means you don't have to spend money cleaning up after a bored, destructive dog.

If your Yorkipoo loves a game of fetch, check out the iFetch Frenzy. Not as high-tech as the original iFetch, which is electronic and can launch a tennis ball up to 30 feet, the iFetch Frenzy uses gravity instead of electricity to drop the ball through one of three holes and send it rolling across the floor. As long as your dog can learn to return the ball to the top, he can play solo fetch for hours while you are away.

Rotate Toys

When you have to leave your Yorkipoo alone for a time, rotate interactive toys that will help to keep him entertained while you are away. Some owners even like to leave the television on while they're gone. There are shows on DogTV that are geared specifically toward dogs that some pooches really seem to enjoy!

CHAPTER 10
Training Your Yorkipoo

"Yorkiooos are extremely smart and learn very quickly. Consistent training will mean your Yorkipoo will learn tasks within just a few repetitions and they'll remember those tricks forever. I have had many Yorkipoos excel in their obedience classes and even in 'trick' classes: complicated classes where they learn to do all kinds of tricks."

JENNIFER EMERT
Jen's Tiny Toys

Benefits of Proper Training

Training your Yorkipoo will deepen the relationship between you and your dog, but it also serves an equally important purpose when it comes to safety. A properly trained Yorkipoo should come when called. This is particularly important in times of crisis or emergency. You should trust that your dog will understand, stay, and obey in stressful situations. That obedience may even save his life.

CELEBRITY YORKIPOOS

Batman Levato

American singer, songwriter, and actress Demi Lovato is the proud owner of a Yorkipoo named Batman. The adorable Yorkipoo was brought into her family in 2015 and, as of 2017, has a puppy sister named Cinderella. The duo once prevented a burglary at Lovato's Los Angeles home when they barked at a burglar who had scaled a ladder to her balcony, alerting the property manager, who was able to prevent the crime.

Yorkipoos love their people and want to obey and make them happy. Your dog only needs to be taught how to do it. There are options when it comes to obedience training. You can search local advertisements and attend a group class, hire a personal trainer to come to your home, or train your dog yourself. No matter what you choose to do, be diligent and stick with the training schedule. The rewards of an obedient Yorkipoo will pay off for years to come.

Training Your Yorkipoo at Home

Whether you choose to handle your dog's training by yourself or hire a personal trainer to come to your home, there are a few things you need to consider. Doing it yourself or hiring a trainer is a great way to fit training into a busy schedule. If you can't make it to obedience classes regularly then a personal trainer may be the best option for you to keep things consistent. Training in your home can also keep your dog safe from any viruses that may possibly be lurking at a training facility that hosts many dogs a week.

One drawback, though, is not seeing how your dog reacts in less than optimal situations. There are many distractions for your dog in a group obedience class but not so many in the quiet of your home. You need your dog to obey in any situation, at home or outside where there are potentially dangerous distractions everywhere. In a group class setting, your dog is learning to be obedient regardless of what is going on around him and this is an invaluable skill.

If you choose to train at home, remember to still occasionally take your dog somewhere else to practice obedience with real-life distractions. If you hire a trainer, ask them how they are making sure to train your dog in all situations and ask about the possibility of taking a training field trip to a public place. This option gives you the best of both worlds with flexibility while also ensuring proper training.

Maintaining Clear Expectations

No matter where you choose to begin obedience training, you should have clear expectations so you can be prepared for the amount of work it will take to successfully train your dog. You play as big a role in obedience training as your dog does, even if you don't choose to do the training yourself.

Obedience classes, either private or group, are usually held about once or twice a week. Check with your vet or groomer for recommendations on trainers. You can also check local listings or find classes at your local pet store.

Most facilities require you to provide vaccination records before classes begin. Obedience training typically begins at about six months of age but dog ages in a class can vary widely. It is never too late to begin obedience training, so even if you have adopted a senior Yorkipoo, he's not too old to learn!

Before your first training session, ask for a list of materials you will need to bring. The facility will likely require your dog to have a leash and

Photo Courtesy of Gwen Anderson

may ask you to provide your own training treats. Most obedience classes require a name tag with identification and some require a clicker. By purchasing all necessary supplies before class day, you can ensure that all your time is spent learning from the trainer and not scrambling to get what you need.

Even if classes are only held twice a week, be prepared to spend at least 15-20 minutes daily working on what your dog has learned. Just as with any skill, obedience training takes practice and repetition. It may not be easy, but through this training your dog will reinforce the idea that you are his pack leader and further prevent "small dog syndrome."

Basic Commands

Obedience training is not just about learning to sit or shake. It is about building trust between you and your Yorkipoo and communicating your wishes in a way your dog can understand. In order to build this trust, though, you must begin by teaching your dog basic commands.

Most obedience classes or personal trainers will begin the training by teaching a few easy, basic commands. These commands lay the foundation for more complicated tricks later. If you are choosing to tackle the job of trainer yourself, remember to keep the training sessions short and positive so your dog does not get frustrated. Follow the steps below to master these five basic commands.

Sit – The sit command is the easiest one to teach and can be learned in a short period of time. Take your dog to a calm area free of distractions like toys. Have a bag full of very small training treats ready. With your dog standing, facing you, hold a treat in front of his nose and slowly raise it up and over his head so he is forced to sit down and look up. Give the verbal command "sit" as you do this. When he sits, reward him with a treat and a key phrase such as "yes" or "good." If you're training with a clicker, also give a click when your dog obeys the command.

Down – Once your dog has mastered the sit command, move to the down command. Guide your dog into a seated position, facing you. Hold a treat in front of his nose, lower it to the floor, and give the verbal command "down." If your dog raises his backside to a standing position to retrieve the treat, take the treat away and calmly say "no." Begin again from a seated position. When your dog successfully lies down to retrieve the treat, reward with a treat, a positive verbal cue such as "yes," and a click.

Heel – Teaching your dog to heel requires him to walk on your left side at your pace whenever you're out and about. The heel command is a bit challenging and requires significant focus from your dog. He must stop when you stop and walk when you walk, never stepping in front of your left heel. This command is great for preventing leash tugging.

Begin by having your dog sit in front, facing you. Using your left hand, let your dog smell the treat and then swing your arm around to the left, luring your dog to turn around and stop in a position next to you but slightly behind, facing the same direction you are. Reward your dog immediately when he arrives in the correct position. Use the command "heel" as he comes into the correct position. Repeat this process many times, always having your dog come to the heel position before rewarding him.

After your dog has mastered the heel position, progress by taking a few steps using the same verbal "heel" command. Reward your dog for walking with you in the correct position. If your dog leaves the correct heel position, guide him back to where he is supposed to be before continuing.

Stay – To teach your dog to stay, command him to sit, facing you. With a visible treat in hand, hold up your palm to your dog and say "stay." Take one step backward. If your dog doesn't move, quickly return to your dog and reward him. You don't want your dog leaving the stay position to retrieve the treat. If your dog moves, say "no" and return him to a sitting position. As your dog gets the hang of "stay," increase the number of steps.

Leave It – This command is invaluable and can help keep your dog safe if he gets into something potentially dangerous. Begin with two treats, one in each hand. Keep one hand in a fist but allow your dog to sniff the treat. As your dog tries to get into your hand to get the treat, verbally command

Photo Courtesy of Minette Ocampo

him to "leave it." Repeat this command until your dog backs off and then reward with the treat from the other hand. As your dog progresses, make the treat more accessible and challenge your pup to leave it in exchange for another treat.

Training Methods

There are two main methods when it comes to training a dog: alpha-dog training and positive reinforcement. Hotly debated among dog trainers, these two methods are vastly different. When choosing the method that is right for your dog, you must take some things into consideration and under-stand the details of each one.

Alpha Dog Training

Alpha training, popularized by dog trainer Cesar Millan, focuses on mak-ing yourself the alpha, or the leader of the pack. This training begins early by maintaining heavy control over your dog's actions. Users of this method are told to never allow your dog in your bed, not let a dog go through a door-way before you do and never get down at eye level with your dog. It is also advised that you touch your dog's food to get your scent on it before giving it to him and don't let him eat until you give the verbal okay.

Proponents of this method claim that dogs are pack animals and need to have a sense of who is alpha in order to learn to submit. They claim that wolves will assert their dominance over one another to keep each other in check and they attempt to achieve the same assertion by using highly con-troversial methods. In reality, research has shown that wolves in the wild actually do not have such a rigid hierarchy. They live socially among each other much like humans do with our own families.

When it comes to obedience training, alpha training employs the use of restraints such as choke and shock collars and forceful body maneuvers. This method relies heavily on punishments and teaching your dog what he is doing wrong rather than teaching him how to do it right. While some trainers believe in the effectiveness of alpha training methods, others believe it is cruel and can actually undermine your relationship with your dog making it one based on fear and not trust.

Dangers of Correcting by Punishment

Correcting by punishment, as used in alpha training, has no scientific research backing it up as a legitimate training method. This type of forced control over a dog can lead to fear and anxiety, especially when used on a small companion dog such as the Yorkipoo. Using this method without an experienced professional's supervision can lead to a damaged relationship with your dog and a loss of trust.

Not only is this type of training risky, but it is also often ineffective. Your dog almost never does anything "bad" intentionally. He is aiming to please and if he is disobedient, it is most likely because he has not been taught what he is supposed to do. By punishing your dog when he does something undesirable, he will often be hurt and confused by what has happened. He may never fully understand which action was the reason for his discomfort in the first place.

Instead of punishing your dog to stop him from doing what he isn't supposed to, show him what he is supposed to do, as discussed in the section on positive reinforcement, and reward him for that. It may take a little bit longer to master but your relationship will grow positively in the process.

Positive Reinforcement

"Positive reinforcement is key, Yorkipoos live to please! Use a calm, assertive, stern voice & body language only to stop them from doing something they shouldn't be doing. Don't forget to let them know when they are doing well also! Get excited and be happy! Show them that! Let them know when they are a good dog!"

MARY LISA CARTER
Sunny Day Puppies

The most recommended method of training today is positive reinforcement. The idea is that by reinforcing good behavior and obedience with desirable treats, your dog will learn the commands and build trust with the trainer. It is still important to let your dog know that you are in control, but this is done through positive reinforcement rather than force. Bad behavior is not punished by harm or discomfort, rather it is ignored or redirected until the positive behavior is consistent.

Dogs have been selectively bred over thousands of years to live alongside humans. Dogs, especially "designer breeds" like the Yorkipoo, thrive on companionship and will do anything to please their people. Using positive reinforcement is a method of teaching them to understand what you want them to do and teaching them that what makes you happy also makes them happy. This is the opposite of fear-based training and will build loyalty and trust naturally.

Primary Reinforcement

Primary reinforcements are directly related to innate, basic needs. These can vary depending on breed and animal but always include things such as food and water. Training treats are a primary reinforcement successfully used in training.

Secondary Reinforcement

Secondary reinforcements are things not based on instinctual, basic need but rather are cultural constructs. This includes verbal praise, smiles, and pats. Your dog must learn to associate these actions positively by pairing them with primary reinforcements.

Another type of secondary reinforcement is conditioned reinforcement. This is when something neutral, such as a whistle or a clicker, is used in conjunction with a primary reinforcement to create a positive association. Conditioned reinforcements can be highly effective initially but can lose their effectiveness when the primary reinforcement is taken away for an extended period of time.

When to Hire a Trainer

If you are attempting to train at home but are having trouble making progress, it may be time to hire a professional trainer. Training a dog takes a lot of time and consistency and it is easy to get frustrated, sending your dog mixed messages while training. If the mixed signals go on for too long, it can actually cause major setbacks in your dog's progress.

If you are dealing with any kind of aggression or poor social behaviors that do not seem to be improving with work, hire a trainer specialized in that area to help you get through to your dog. Be sure, before you hire a trainer, that they train using positive reinforcement methods. A successful trainer should have many previous clients willing to testify to a positive experience.

If you think you need help from a professional trainer, don't put it off. The sooner your dog is properly trained, the sooner you can live together in peaceful companionship.

CHAPTER 11
Traveling with Your Yorkipoo

"Most Yorkipoos love to travel but some get carsick. Practice short rides at first starting in your driveway & advancing as slow as possible to encourage them to enjoy traveling. You may even use cerenia (carsick preventative medicine from your vet) to help. Traveling will never be fun for your dog if they get carsick."

MARY LISA CARTER
Sunny Day Puppies

Deciding whether or not to travel with your Yorkipoo can be a tough decision. We all want to take our fluffy companions with us wherever we go but traveling can put unneeded stress on a dog. This chapter will explain all the ins and outs of traveling with your Yorkipoo so you can make the best decision for you and your dog. For more information on specifically traveling with your dog by car, see Chapter 4.

Photo Courtesy
of Bianca Jacques

Photo Courtesy of Mollie Chapman

Flying with Your Dog

No matter how small he is or how easy it may seem to let him tag along on all of your adventures, flying with your Yorkipoo will take a lot of planning beforehand. There are only so many pets allowed on each airplane (this varies by airline and size of the plane), so you need to book your flight as early as possible to obtain a spot. In the past, airlines treated cargo animals just like any other luggage. Dogs were often left traumatized and sometimes even died because of high or low temperatures, lack of water, etc. Luckily, today, airlines have begun enforcing regulations to keep animals housed in the cargo area as safe and happy as possible.

Due to the size of a Yorkipoo, your dog will most likely be able to board the plane with you in the cabin. Of course, all airlines have different rules and they are constantly changing, so it's best to check directly with your airline before purchasing your ticket.

Flying with your beloved pooch won't come cheap, however. Most airlines charge anywhere from $100-$125 each way. Depending on the airline, your pup will have to fit into a small, well-ventilated carrier that will fit below your seat by your feet for the duration of the flight. Again, check specifically with your airline for these regulations as they all vary slightly.

Not all airlines follow the same guidelines for flying animals. Some require a certificate of veterinary inspection (CVI) and certain vaccines before flying. Make sure you do thorough research on each airline before deciding on the best for you and your Yorkipoo. Federal regulations prohibit any pets under eight weeks old from flying.

Photo Courtesy of Denise Murphy

Hotel Stays with Your Dog

If you plan to stay in a hotel with your dog, there are a few things you need to look for before choosing. Not all hotels are pet friendly, and some have size and breed restrictions. Before booking, check the hotel's website to be sure that dogs are allowed. Checking online for the highest rated pet-friendly hotels is a great place to start.

FUN FACT
Yorkipoos Are the Most Adorable Dogs

Littlethings.com, an uplifting online publishing platform, ranked Yorkipoos as the ninth most adorable small dog breed. The article, written by Stephanie Kaloi, also names Yorkies (thirteenth place) and Pekingese (first place) to the list.

When deciding on a hotel, make sure it has adequate outdoor space for your Yorkipoo. Not all hotels allow pets, and, even then, a hotel may consider itself "pet-friendly" but may not have much to offer in the way of pet amenities. Although your Yorkipoo doesn't need much outdoor space, he will need a place to do his business comfortably.

You may also want to request a room on the ground floor. This will make it easier for you to access the bathroom area designated for your dog. Some hotels are known for designating the older, outdated, or smoking rooms as pet rooms. Before booking, call and ask if the pet rooms are any different from other rooms.

Bring a kennel when staying in a hotel just in case you have to leave your Yorkipoo for any period of time. Some hotels don't allow pets to be left alone, so make sure you check beforehand. Even if you don't plan on using the kennel, you never know when something might come up, and you don't want your dog to cause any damage in the room if left alone.

Kenneling vs. Dog-Sitters

If you are choosing to travel without your dog, there are several choices for care while you are gone. You can put your dog at a boarding kennel until you return, or you can hire a dog-sitter. Depending on your needs and the personality of your dog, either of these can be a great option. You can also ask a family member or friend to care for your dog while you are away. Just be sure they are responsible and care for your pooch as much as you do!

If you won't be gone for an extended period, you might find hiring a dog-sitter a more affordable option. This is typically when you hire someone

Photo Courtesy
of Dawn Phillips

to come and take your dog out 2-3 times a day and make sure he has food and water. You could find a sitter through online resources such as pet-sitter.com, or you may ask a reliable friend or relative to do this. Because Yorkipoos require constant companionship and suffer when alone, this is only a good option for a day or two. After this, your dog may begin to feel cooped up and anxious, possibly becoming destructive.

You can also hire a 24-hour dog-sitter who will stay overnight to care for your dog. This will, of course, be a more expensive option. It would allow your dog to have companionship and constant care, however.

Finding a good boarding kennel is the best option because it prevents your dog from being left alone. Most of these places allow your dog to play with other dogs in a safe environment for most of the day. A stay at a boarding kennel can be like a vacation for your dog!

Choosing the Right Boarding Facility

All boarding facilities are different and come with their own rules and benefits. They can range from basic, small, cage-like kennels to full-sized dog rooms with elevated beds and doggy doors to an outside patio. Nice boarding facilities will have a common area inside and out where the dogs can play together. Price can vary drastically depending on location but can range between $20 and $60 a night.

Never take your dog to a boarder that does not require the Bordetella vaccine. These places can be a breeding ground for kennel cough, so make sure you plan for your dog to get the vaccine at least two weeks before his visit.

Check out local boarding facilities online before choosing and check consumer reviews. Ask your local pet store or vet and see which they do and don't recommend. Most facilities charge a price per night and will often have different levels of service. Oftentimes, these places will allow you to choose between a private or shared room, and some even have televisions with DogTV. You may even be able to watch a live stream of your Yorkipoo while he is playing with his new buddies.

Whichever route you choose, make sure you trust your choice and that your dog is well taken care of while you are away. The last thing you want to do is worry about your dog while you are away.

Photo Courtesy
of Nora Larkins

Special Tips and Tricks for Traveling

Traveling with your Yorkipoo can be fun and exciting, but it can also be stressful! Follow these tips to help any trip with your little companion be a stress-free one.

- Don't feed your dog within four hours of any trip. This includes car rides, plane rides, and any other method of transportation. This may help prevent your having to clean up vomit.

- Exercise your Yorkipoo vigorously the day before and the day of your trip. Let him get as much energy out as he possibly can before being put into his carrier.

- Don't sedate your dog! This once common practice is no longer recommended by veterinarians. Sedating a dog can inhibit his ability to react in an emergency and is simply not good for his health.
- Check in as late as possible at the airport so that your dog doesn't have to spend the extra time waiting.
- If you are flying, make sure that your rental car or car service allows for dogs to ride.
- Always have a bowl, leash, water, and plastic waste bags with you. No matter how you are traveling, these basic items will be daily necessities. If you're driving, use a safety harness as discussed earlier, and stop often to let your dog potty and drink water.
- Always have the number to a local emergency vet on hand. Emergencies can happen anywhere, so look up local animal hospitals before you travel—just in case!

CHAPTER 12
Grooming Your Yorkipoo

Coat Basics

The Yorkipoo possesses a low-dander, non-shedding coat. However, because the Yorkipoo is a cross breed and there is no standard for appearance, their coats will vary a bit from dog to dog.

There are three basic coat types that your Yorkipoo may have:

Curly – A Yorkipoo with a curly coat has inherited more of a Poodle-type coat.

Straight – A Yorkipoo with a straight coat has taken on more of the Yorkshire Terrier characteristics. These coats are typically finer and silkier than their curly or wavy counterparts.

Wavy – Probably the most common Yorkipoo coat, wavy coats are a result of the combination of the two parent coat types.

Regardless of your pup's coat type, this chapter will take you through all the grooming basics you need to know to properly care for your Yorkipoo and his beautiful coat.

Photo Courtesy of Christine Schatz

Basic Grooming Tools

The majority of your investment in grooming your Yorkipoo will be spent in time maintaining his coat. With just a basic set of brushes, scissors, and shampoo, you will have all you need to keep your Yorkipoo looking great. If you choose to clip your dog at home instead of the groomer, which we will discuss later in this chapter, you will also need to invest in a quality set of dog clippers. Aside from coat care, you will also need to have nail trimmers, styptic powder, a dog toothbrush, toothpaste, and ear and eye wash.

FUN FACT
Toy or Miniature

Yorkipoos are a mixed-breed dog resulting from a Yorkshire Terrier and either a Miniature or Toy Poodle. A Yorkipoo bred from a Yorkie and a Miniature Poodle will likely grow to be larger than one who is bred from a Yorkie and a Toy Poodle. Toy Poodles range from around 9.5 to eleven inches tall, while Miniature Poodles average a height of fifteen inches. Yorkies average a height of eight or nine inches, smaller than both Toy and Miniature Poodles.

Bathing and Brushing

Regular brushing and baths are the key to keeping your dog's coat looking clean and healthy. Brushing is required at least on a weekly basis to prevent matting. Bathing, on the other hand, should only happen a maximum of once a month to prevent skin issues. Bathing your Yorkipoo too often will strip the oils from his skin and cause dryness.

Before bathing your Yorkipoo, use a blow dryer to blow any excess dirt or hair off his coat. Keep the dryer far enough off the coat to avoid causing tangles and burning his skin. After this, proceed with shampooing your dog.

When shampooing your Yorkipoo, you will want to use a quality dog shampoo. Ask local vets and groomers what they recommend. Never use human shampoo or conditioner on your dog. Shampoo is largely chosen based on personal preference so you may have to try a few out before finding one that is just right for you and your Yorkipoo.

Whichever shampoo you choose, make sure it is free from parabens, dyes, sulfates, and DEA. These are ingredients commonly used in commercial shampoos but are known to have potentially damaging effects over time. It is also best to avoid any added fragrances, especially if your dog has sensitive skin.

It is best to bathe your dog in a tub or sink with a hand sprayer, but a large rinsing cup will do if that is all you have. Make sure you clean the coat all the way down to the skin, using your fingers to scrub and massage the skin. Rinse with cool water and then use a towel to blot dry. Don't use the towel to rub your dog dry because this will cause tangles and mats to form in the dog's coat.

Finish drying with a hairdryer, using the same precautions to prevent tangles and burning as mentioned before, and use the bristle brush to remove

Photo Courtesy
of Bianca Jacques

any tangles that have occurred. Once finished, check the consistency of the coat with your hands. If one area feels denser, go back over that area with the brush to remove any mats.

Finding a grooming brush for your Yorkipoo can easily become overwhelming because there are so many types of brushes all created for different purposes and coat types. Since Yorkipoos are prone to tangles and mats, regardless of their coat type, you will want to purchase a slicker brush. These are usually flat with short, fine wire bristles.

The slicker brush is used for removing mats and tangles and should be used at least once a week. When using the slicker brush, make short, controlled movements to avoid causing breakage and static. Make sure you get the brush all the way to the hair shaft at the skin.

YORKIPOOS IN THE NEWS

Pennsylvania Pet of the Week

Riley the Yorkipoo was voted Lebanon County's Pet of the Week by LebTown magazine in October 2020. Riley was adopted from the Humane Society when he was three years old and is owned by McKenzie Hall. Riley enjoys naps, attention, and going for walks. LebTown Pets of the Week are nominated by their owners, and the weekly feature aims to help the community start each week with "the best vibes possible." Adorable Yorkipoos seem like the best way to start any week!

You will also want to purchase a natural bristle brush as a finishing brush to give your Yorkipoo a once-over after using the slicker brush. These brushes have tightly packed natural bristles and help to stimulate the skin's oils, keeping your Yorkipoo's coat shiny and healthy.

Nail Trimming

Some people opt to have a groomer or a veterinarian trim their dog's nails, but you can easily do this at home. There are several types of quality nail trimmers to choose from, but they will all get the job done so choose based on your preference and what is easiest for you to maneuver. You should also purchase some styptic powder. This will stop any bleeding if you accidentally cut a nail too short. Most clippers will come with instructions on how to clip the nails and it is important to follow them carefully to avoid injury to your dog.

Introduce the nail clippers to your Yorkipoo early and often. Let your dog explore and sniff the clippers so he can get familiar with them. Hold them down to his feet and show him that they are not a threat. Reward him with treats to create a positive association. Do this often, even when your Yorkipoo doesn't need a nail trim. This will help him to stay relaxed when it is time for an actual nail trimming session.

A dog's nail is made up of the nail and the quick. The quick is the pink part inside the nail. If your dog has light-colored nails, the quick may be visible making it easier to avoid. If the nails are black you will not be able to see the quick and will need to be extra cautious not to trim too far back. If you do hit the quick, this is called quicking and is a very painful experience for your dog. It will bleed a lot so immediately apply styptic powder.

The two most common types of nail trimmers are the guillotine type and the scissor type. To use the guillotine or scissor trimmers, carefully place the

*Photo Courtesy
of Jennifer Nelson*

dogs nail into the clipper and cut at a 45-degree angle away from the pad. Remember, the longer a dog's nails, the longer the blood supply is inside the nail, so only trim a little at a time, even if your dog's nails are overgrown. As the nail is trimmed shorter, the blood supply will also retreat, making it possible to shorten his nails over time. Trim a small amount every ten days or so until the nails are the length you want. If you do cause bleeding, stop it immediately with styptic powder.

Cleaning the Ears and Eyes

You should clean your Yorkipoo's ears weekly in order to prevent infections. To do this, gently squeeze one ear with cleaning solution as directed on the bottle. Massage the ear canal and then move on to the other ear. Shaking his head afterward is normal and completely fine! Unless your dog is particularly cooperative, you will need someone to help you hold your dog while you put the liquid in his ear.

You may also want to regularly flush your Yorkipoo's eyes if you find they are prone to catching dirt and debris. Do this by using a dog eye wash and dropping the recommended number of drops directly into the eye. Consult the directions on the bottle to know how often you should flush your dog's eyes.

Regularly trimming the hair on a Yorkipoo's face in between his eyes is a must to prevent catching more debris and blocking vision. Do this very carefully with a pair of dog shears or take your dog to the groomer every three weeks for a face trim. Never attempt to trim the hair between a dog's eyes if your dog is upset and nervous. One wrong movement and serious injury could occur for your beloved pup.

Dental Care

Dental health is often overlooked when it comes to dogs, but proper oral care is important! Dogs can suffer from the same oral diseases and pains that humans do. Your dog should be taken to the vet every year or two for a professional dental cleaning. Talk to your vet about how often he or she recommends.

At home, brush your dog's teeth with a dog-specific toothbrush and toothpaste often to prevent any oral issues down the road. Never use human toothpaste, which is full of additives that are meant to be spit out and not swallowed. Brush gently and take it slow until your dog is accustomed to the toothbrush. Begin with the toothpaste on your finger if he doesn't take well

*Photo Courtesy
of Nancy Coogan*

to the brush. It is a good idea to do this at the same time you brush his coat every week to create a routine.

Brushing is not the only way to help your Yorkipoo keep his teeth in tip-top shape. Chewing has been shown to naturally reduce plaque and tartar build-up. Dental chews come in many sizes, so just make sure you get the right size for your little Yorkipoo. When using these, it is advisable to have your dog on your lap and hold one end of the chew in your hand as he enjoys the chomping. This will ensure that your precious pup does not try to swallow a piece that is too big for him and might cause choking.

Should I Clip at Home and When to Seek Professional Help

It is very important to keep up with a regular grooming routine. It is not recommended you try to trim your Yorkipoo's hair at home, but, instead, hire a professional groomer to make sure the job is done properly. Your Yorkipoo will need to visit the groomer for a full clip every 6-8 weeks.

While some may try to attempt the clippers at home, it is not as easy as a trained groomer may make it look. These at-home grooming sessions almost always take hours and ultimately end up back in the groomer to fix whatever went wrong. Save yourself time and effort and let the professional care for your dog's coat.

Choosing a Groomer

When choosing a groomer to care for your Yorkipoo, first ask friends and family who they use for their dog's grooming needs. Personal recommendations are the best way to find a reputable groomer who cares for the dogs and produces quality cuts.

If you cannot find a reputable groomer by word of mouth, check local reviews online. You may even want to call and request a tour of your favorites so you can see how they work and care for the dogs firsthand. Cleanliness should be a priority in the grooming facility. If it's not, walk away and keep looking.

A reputable groomer should also be able to show you his previous work through photos. If he cannot, this would be a major red flag and a reason to move on to the next groomer.

Whatever method of grooming you choose, do not ever neglect your Yorkipoo's grooming needs, or you may find that it can get out of hand quickly and will become a much bigger job.

CHAPTER 13
Basic Health Care

Visiting the Vet

Aside from the first vet visit discussed in Chapter 4, your Yorkipoo should see the vet routinely for check-ups and vaccinations. At these regular visits, your vet will give your dog a good look over to make sure the pup is healthy. The vet should listen to your dog's heart and lungs and examine the ears, eyes, nose, and mouth. The visit should also include an abdominal examination, looking for any abnormalities.

The vet may also draw blood to check for heartworms and take a stool sample to check for other parasites. Sometimes the vet will examine your dog's gait and coat condition. Be ready to answer questions about diet or other routines for your Yorkipoo. Like most dog breeds, Yorkipoos are susceptible to a few genetic conditions, so it is important to keep up with annual wellness checks with your vet so that you can catch anything early before it becomes a bigger issue.

Photo Courtesy
of Niki Gordon

Fleas and Ticks

Fleas are the most common external parasite to afflict dogs, and they are a problem almost everywhere. They reproduce quickly, and a single female flea can lay 20-40 eggs a day. If your dog picks up a flea or two from the park and he has not been protected, you could be dealing with an infestation in your home before you know it.

Ticks can go largely unnoticed by their host, but they can cause a much bigger health problem than fleas. Ticks are notorious for transmitting dangerous diseases to dogs, humans, and other animals. While most ticks will prefer your furry friend as a host, they won't hesitate to latch on to you if given the opportunity.

FUN FACT
Wisdom Panel 4.0

A new DNA test for pets has hit the market and is designed for dog owners to learn more about their dogs. Wisdom Panel 4.0 can give information about the past three generations of your dog's family tree. Michelle Castillo, a reporter for CNBC Digital, decided to run the DNA test for her nine-year-old pup, Roscoe, who she suspected was a Yorkipoo. The test was able to pinpoint Roscoe's heritage and gave Castillo an indication of which percentage of poodle and Yorkie Roscoe possesses!

Flea and tick prevention is important for your Yorkipoo's health and for your own. There are many options when it comes to prevention, and it is important to understand the benefits and the disadvantages before you choose the treatment that is best for your dog.

A common type of flea and tick preventative is one that is administered topically. Typically, this medication comes in a small tube that the owner squeezes onto the dog's back between the shoulder blades. This topical medication usually takes about 12 hours to take effect and will last about 30 days before it needs to be reapplied. The solution is absorbed into the skin and circulates through the dog's bloodstream, treating fleas and ticks over the entire body, not just the area it was applied. One disadvantage of this application is it usually leaves a greasy spot on your dog's back for a few days. Considering this is a medication, it is probably not something you want to touch yourself or allow children to come in contact with.

There is usually a minimum age requirement for these medications, so it is best to consult your vet before applying topical flea treatments to a young dog.

Another method of administration is oral medication. There are numerous tablets on the market that prevent fleas and ticks for 30 days. Some of these prevent heartworms and internal parasites as well. Depending on how your dog takes medication, this could be an easier way to prevent the parasites without the mess of topical medication. Just as with any medications, side effects do exist. While they are generally mild, some dogs can react with skin irritations, vomiting, or diarrhea to oral flea preventatives.

You can also buy a special flea collar for your dog. These are collars worn in addition to your dog's identification collar. They are covered with topical flea medications, usually permethrin. This provides up to eight months protection for your dog but can also cause skin irritation. While these collars have been deemed safe for dogs, permethrin can cause toxicity in cats. Just like with the topical medication, children and adults should avoid contact with the active ingredients on flea collars. As with topical medications, flea collars should never be used on a young puppy, and the same precautions should be taken.

Even though your Yorkipoo will live primarily inside, he should always be on a flea and tick preventative. It is much better to take preventative measures than to have to deal with the fleas or ticks after they have hitched a ride into your home.

Photo Courtesy of Michael Rose

If you suspect your dog might have fleas, you can purchase a flea comb at any pet store. Flea combs have very fine and closely spaced teeth that fleas cannot pass between. Run the flea comb over your dog's body at a 45-degree angle, focusing on the head, neck, and hindquarters. If you see a flea in the comb, cover it quickly and trap it in a wet paper towel. Drop the flea in a bowl of soapy water to kill it.

You may also give your dog a flea bath. Vacuum your entire house from the floor to the curtains. Anything upholstered is potentially a place where a flea has laid eggs. If you notice fleas in your home, continue vacuuming twice a day for two weeks in order to get rid of all the fleas as they hatch.

If you find a tick on your dog, remove it immediately. Always wear gloves when removing a tick. Ticks carry serious diseases, and you don't want to come into contact with their saliva or risk being bitten yourself. Once you have your gloves on, use a clean pair of tweezers and grab the tick firmly as close to the skin as possible. Pull firmly, straight up. You don't want to leave any of the tick's mouthparts behind, or this could lead to infection. Once you have removed the tick, place it in a jar of alcohol or soapy water. Clean the bite thoroughly with antiseptic and watch the area for signs of irritation. Keep the tick for identification in case your dog shows any symptoms of illness. Symptoms can take two weeks to surface, so watch your Yorkipoo carefully.

Worms and Parasites

There are a number of intestinal worms and parasites that can wreak havoc on your dog's health if left untreated. These include hookworms, ringworms, roundworms, tapeworms, whipworms, coccidia, giardia, and spirochetes. A vet typically diagnoses these parasites through a stool sample, but there are particular symptoms you can watch for.

Hookworm – Hookworm larvae live in the soil and can be picked up by your Yorkipoo through common activities. These parasites attach themselves to the intestinal walls and feed off the dog's blood. As with most parasites, puppies are most susceptible to hookworms. Diarrhea and weight loss can be signs of possible hookworm infestation, which requires a vet diagnosis.

Once diagnosed, hookworms can be treated with an oral medication. Depending on the severity, iron supplements may be needed to treat anemia. Humans can also contract hookworms, often by walking barefoot on soil contaminated with feces. Symptoms include abdominal pain, intestinal cramps, nausea, fever, blood in stool and a rash. More common in developing nations, humans rarely contract hookworms in the United States.

Ringworm – Ringworm is actually a fungus, not a worm, and it causes circular bald patches on your dog's skin. This condition is easily spread and mostly affects dogs with compromised immune systems, including young puppies and elderly dogs. Depending on the severity of the infection, your vet will likely treat your dog with a medicated shampoo and possibly an oral medication.

Roundworm – Roundworms are extremely common in dogs and are usually discovered when an owner spots a round, white worm, an inch or two in length, in their dog's stool. There are other symptoms to keep an eye out for, such as coughing, vomiting, diarrhea, and weight loss; however, these only present in severe cases. Ringworms can also be passed to humans, especially children.

Tapeworm – A dog can get tapeworms when it accidentally ingests parasite larvae, oftentimes by eating a flea. Weight loss and diarrhea are common symptoms of tapeworm, as are small worm segments resembling grains of rice in your dog's stool. Treatment for tapeworms involves oral medication and sometimes injections as well.

Whipworm – Unlike other intestinal parasites, whipworms are difficult to spot in a stool sample. These worms live in the large intestine and cause weight loss in dogs. A sign of infection may be a mucous covering at the tip of your dog's stool. While whipworm infection is not typically serious, oral medication is required to eradicate them.

Photo Courtesy of Jean Reilly

Coccidia, Giardia, and Spirochetes – These are not worms but are single-celled parasites that can do much damage to your dog before you even know he is infected. These parasites can cause lasting diseases and issues for a dog and require swift treatment from a vet. Often transmitted through water, food, soil, and feces, these parasites live in unsanitary conditions. Young puppies and older dogs are more susceptible to these, due to their weakened immune systems.

Medication to treat these parasites is typically given orally. The severity of the case will determine the length of time these medications will need to be taken.

Vaccinations

Vaccinations prevent diseases by injecting the body with antigens to elicit an immune response producing antibodies for those diseases. The vaccinations cause no symptoms of disease but give the dog's body time to build up an immunity so that if the dog comes into contact with a virus, his immune system will respond fast enough to shorten the illness significantly. Vaccinations are an important part of keeping your dog healthy and safe from potentially life-threatening illnesses.

A puppy will receive antibodies from its mother's milk for at least the first six weeks of its life and should be protected from many illnesses that way. Distemper, Adenovirus, Hepatitis, Parvovirus, and Parainfluenza are considered the core vaccinations that every puppy should receive at six weeks of age. These shots are usually given in four rounds: once at six weeks, ten weeks, fourteen weeks, and eighteen weeks. Most vets administer these core shots in a combination vaccine called a 5-Way. Depending on your area, some vets will recommend additional vaccinations. These may include Bordetella, Leptospirosis, and Coronavirus.

The rabies vaccine is always administered separately and is recommended no earlier than 12 weeks. Some veterinarians may want to give it in addition to other combo vaccinations at your Yorkipoo's second-round appointment. Depending on where you live, legally, your dog will have to receive a rabies vaccine every one to three years.

Reactions to these vaccines are rare but possible. Sometimes vaccinations can trigger an allergic reaction causing swelling, hives, vomiting, and fever. If your dog does have a reaction, notify your vet immediately. Even if the reaction is mild, make sure the vet is aware before your dog is given more vaccinations. The benefits of vaccinations far outweigh the risks. They are one of the best ways to help set your dog up for a long, healthy life.

Common Diseases and Conditions in Yorkipoos

Genetic conditions that often plague pure-bred dogs are typically lessened, or eliminated, by crossbreeding. This makes your Yorkipoo, in general, a pretty healthy dog! Although he is less likely to suffer from the genetic conditions that affect his purebred parents, it's important to understand the common diseases that can afflict Yorkipoos, so you can be prepared in any event.

Hypoglycemia – Yorkipoos are prone to hypoglycemia, which is an abnormally low blood sugar level. Symptoms of this condition are lethargy, weakness, and fainting. This is most likely to affect dogs within the first 5 months of life, but can happen at any age. If you notice any symptoms of hypoglycemia, giving your Yorkipoo a fingerful of honey can be a temporary fix, but you must contact your vet right away for long-term solutions and monitoring.

Kneecap Dislocation – An issue more common in very small dogs, kneecap dislocation can occur occasionally in Yorkipoos. This condition often corrects itself when the kneecap "pops" back into place. Your dog will probably let out a yelp and limp for a few minutes if this happens. If this becomes an issue for your Yorkipoo, surgical correction may be an option.

Collapsing Trachea – Another common ailment in very small dogs, a collapsing trachea occurs because the trachea of the Yorkipoo is narrower than normal. This condition is evident by symptoms such as coughing, gagging, gasping for breath, and noisy breathing.

Prevent this condition by avoiding anything that will tug or put resistance on your Yorkipoo's neck and throat. Always attach a leash to a harness and not a collar.

Hip Dysplasia – Hip dysplasia is a condition in which the ball and socket of the hip joint do not grow at the same rate. This abnormal formation

Photo Courtesy of Minette Ocampo

causes a looseness of the joint which may lead to pain and even lameness. Usually not diagnosed until two years of age, hip dysplasia is not a life-threatening disease but can greatly reduce the quality of a dog's life. Sometimes, hip dysplasia can be managed with drugs, weight control, and monitored exercise. A Yorkipoo with severe hip dysplasia may need surgery to attempt to repair or replace the hip altogether.

Legg-Perthes Disease – A disease somewhat similar to hip dysplasia, Legg-Perthes Disease causes the ball of the hip joint to physically deteriorate. Symptoms of this condition include limping, which usually happens gradually, over a period of weeks but can sometimes come on suddenly. Usually only affecting one of the back legs, this condition is typically apparent within the first year of a dog's life.

Because this condition often leads to lameness, contact your vet immediately if your dog is limping or resisting putting weight on one of his back legs. X-rays can confirm a diagnosis. In mild cases, therapy can ease pain along with medication. In severe cases, surgery to remove or replace the head of the femur may be required.

Portosystemic Shunt – This genetic disease is caused by an abnormality in the portal vein in the abdomen. This causes some of the dog's blood to bypass the liver and pump into the body, delivering toxins to major organs. Symptoms of the condition include loss of coordination, poor muscle development, vomiting, diarrhea, loss of cognitive function, excessive drooling.

This condition is diagnosed with a blood test. Once confirmed, surgery to repair the portal vein is the best option. Diet restriction and medications as prescribed by your vet may also help.

Other Notable Diseases – Yorkipoos may be affected by eye conditions such as retinal dysplasia. Immune disorders are also possible, including allergies, thyroid conditions, cancer, and other autoimmune disorders.

Holistic Alternatives and Supplements

If your pet has developed a medical condition, or if you want to take every precaution to prevent or delay one, the first step toward health and wellness for your Yorkipoo should be a healthy diet. Dogs should have a high-protein diet limiting wheat, corn, and soy. Consider skipping the kibble and making your dog a homemade, nutrition-packed meal. The next chapter discusses nutrition and dog food alternatives.

Acupuncture

Acupuncture, which involves pricking the skin or tissues with needles, is becoming more common in pets because of its notable benefits in managing pain and increasing circulation. Supporting overall wellness, acupuncture can aid in the treatment of hip dysplasia, allergies, gastrointestinal problems, and pain due to cancer treatments. Acupuncture causes no pain and is shown to have a calming effect in pets. You should always consult your veterinarian before beginning any alternative treatments. Acupuncture should only be performed by a certified acupuncturist.

Herbs

Herbs are a staple in holistic health care, but not all herbs are safe for dogs, and some can interact with medications your dog may be taking. Discuss any herbs with your vet before adding them to your dog's diet or lifestyle. Some herbs include:

Goldenseal. Anti-inflammatory and anti-bacterial, goldenseal can be used externally on bodily infections or as an eyewash for infections or conjunctivitis. It can be taken internally at the first sign of kennel cough or digestive issues and can also be beneficial in the treatment of tapeworms and Giardia. Goldenseal should not be used for too long as it can cause stress on the liver.

Milk Thistle. Milk thistle provides liver support by protecting against damage. If your dog is on any medication that can damage his liver, discuss adding milk thistle to his regimen with your vet.

Ginger. Just as with people, ginger is an effective tool for treating nausea and cardiovascular conditions in dogs. Ginger has cardiotonic effects and can promote functionality of the heart.

Chamomile. Another herb that aids digestion, relieves muscle spasms, and reduces inflammation, chamomile is a great option for treating chronic bowel and gas disorders and can also ease your Yorkipoo's anxiety.

Licorice. Licorice root is a fast-acting anti-inflammatory that can be used to treat arthritis and other inflammatory diseases. It has been shown to enhance the efficacy of other herbs, so it is often combined with others as a part of a treatment plan.

CBD Oil. Per the American Kennel Club's website, "Currently, there has been no formal study on how CBD affects dogs. What scientists do know is that cannabinoids interact with the endocannabinoid receptors located in the central and peripheral nervous systems, which help maintain balance in the body and keep it in a normal healthy state."

CBD oil, also known as cannabidiol, is thought to treat pain and help control seizures in dogs. Anecdotal evidence also shows that CBD oil may have anti-inflammatory, anti-cancer, anti-anxiety, and cardiac benefits. Discuss with your vet the option of adding a CBD supplement to your dog's lifestyle.

These are only a few of the herbs available for homeopathic use for your dog. If you want your dog to experience the benefits of herbal remedies but can't source the herbs yourself, there are many pre-made solutions and tinc-tures available for the holistic care of your Yorkipoo. They come conveniently packaged and mixed with directions so you can know you are using the herb correctly. Be sure to only use products from a reputable source with a reputation for supplying the best holistic and herbal treatments. Beware of cheaper products that may contain synthetics. And always consult your vet before beginning any herbal treatment for your Yorkipoo.

Pet Insurance

Some pet owners choose to invest in pet insurance in the event any conditions arise. It is advisable to carefully research each provider to weigh costs versus benefits before taking out a policy. Different companies offer different coverage, so be sure to read the fine print and understand any exclusions. Talk with your vet to see if he has a company he recommends.

Rates will vary based on your dog's age, history, and condition. While it is generally considered more affordable to pay out of pocket for vet visits for common ailments, pet insurance can be a life-saver if something cata-strophic arises, and your Yorkipoo needs expensive tests or surgery, or will require medication for life.

CHAPTER 14
Nutrition

Benefits of Quality Dog Food

For the sake of our health, we do our best to eat a balanced diet and avoid processed foods with harmful additives. These same rules apply when it comes to feeding our dogs. Just like humans, dogs need a certain balance of protein, fats, carbohydrates, vitamins, and minerals to stay healthy.

All commercial dog foods have been tested rigorously and are required to meet minimum nutritional requirements. However, minimum requirements are not what is best for your dog's health long-term. Feeding your dog low-quality food is the equivalent of feeding him junk food. Choosing a dog food that is made with the best ingredients and which does not include preservatives and additives will help your dog function at his optimal level, potentially protecting him against disease.

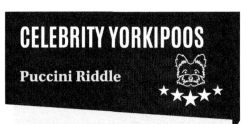

CELEBRITY YORKIPOOS

Puccini Riddle

★★★★★

Leslie Riddle, a former Miss Texas Teen and Radio City Music Hall Rockette, competed in the first-ever Dog Mom USA pageant alongside her Yorkipoo named Puccini in 2019. Puccini, who was eleven years old at the time of the pageant, is a rescue and was voted "Most Photogenic" at an annual dog show in the Hamptons called Barking Beauties. For the final pageant segment, Puccini sported a silver suit to coordinate with his mom's floor-length ball gown.

According to Dr. Hugh Stevenson, a veterinarian in Ontario, Canada for over twenty years, symptoms of poor nutrition include a dull, thin coat, poor quality footpads (which can crack or bleed), weight problems, excess stool and gas, and passing undigested grain particles in feces. Quality dog nutrition leads to a lustrous coat, healthy skin and weight, and less stool due to more of the food being digestible. When it comes to your lovable Yorkipoo companion, quality food will give him the best possible start in life from puppyhood on.

Photo Courtesy
of Ruth Llewellyn

Types of Commercial Dog Foods

There are many dog foods that claim to be the best, healthiest, and most complete. It can be both overwhelming and confusing. Should you buy dry kibble? Canned wet food? Each contains a different list of ingredients and promises on the label. So how do you really know what you're getting?

The first choice you will have to make is whether to feed your dog dry kibble or wet food. Each choice comes with its own set of positives and negatives.

Wet Dog Food – Wet dog food has a very strong smell. This may be a positive for a dog who is particularly picky or doesn't have much interest in eating, as the strong scent may entice him to eat. It could also be a negative if you don't want to smell the food in your home every time you feed your dog.

Wet food also helps with hydration if you have a dog that doesn't drink as much as he should, but it spoils quickly after opening. If your dog doesn't finish his food promptly, you'll need to store the rest in the refrigerator. Canned food can also be a bit messier to eat, depending on your dog.

Dry Dog Food – Dry dog food doesn't spoil when left out. This is beneficial for a dog who may like to come back to his food and finish later. Dry dog food also doesn't have much of a smell, so it can sit out without anyone noticing. Some dry kibble is formulated to help clean your dog's teeth while he chews, although some experts say the added grains in certain dry foods contribute to tooth decay.

Whichever type of food you choose for your dog, it's important to remember that both canned food and kibble exist in low-quality forms. Low-quality brands include cheap fillers, artificial colors and flavors, and preservatives and should be avoided.

Ingredients to Watch Out For

"Variety of diet is as important for them as it is for us humans. Read the ingredients on your foods and do some research. Meat is important of course & naturally added vitamins/minerals instead of chemically added is always better. Do NOT feed treats that are not SOURCED in the USA. 'Made in the USA' does not cut the cheese."

MARY LISA CARTER
Sunny Day Puppies

It can be confusing reading the ingredient list on a dog food label. Companies that produce low-quality dog food use vague terms and scientific words to try and make you think the product contains quality, wholesome ingredients, when it may not. Below is a list of key ingredients to avoid when searching for the best commercial dog food for your Yorkipoo.

BHA/ BHT – Studies are not conclusive, but these chemical preservatives have been linked to hyperactivity and cancer. Used to preserve fats in human food and pet food, BHA and BHT have been banned in some countries but are still allowed in the United States, Canada, and Europe. Until conclusive evidence proves these preservatives are safe, it's best to avoid them altogether.

Meat, Meat Meal, or Rendered Fat – Any time you see a vague, non-specific term such as "meat" or "meat meal," you can bet these are the lowest quality ingredients allowed. These ingredients are leftovers from slaughterhouses—the parts humans won't eat. It can also include leftover, expired meats from the grocery store and diseased or dying livestock. Look for specific meat terms you recognize on your dog's food, such as turkey, beef, salmon, lamb, or chicken.

If your dog food contains salmon or salmon meal, make sure it's labeled "wild-caught." Farm-raised salmon is less nutrient-dense than its wild counterpart because of the unnatural diet the fish are fed and has been found to potentially contain more contaminants.

Nitrites and Nitrates – Chemical additives used to preserve freshness and extend the shelf life of meat products, nitrates and nitrites are found in human and dog food. Sodium nitrite can be toxic to your dog in high doses and has been linked to cancer.

Soy – Soy is cheap and readily available. Dog food manufacturers may use it as an inexpensive way to boost the protein percentage of the food, but it can be difficult for your dog to digest and can cause gastrointestinal upset.

Other ingredients to avoid include meat by-products, sodium hexametaphosphate, food dyes, carrageenan, taurine, cellulose, artificial flavors, and

Photo Courtesy of Julie Gigliotti

corn syrup. Dog food manufacturers dedicated to producing a quality, superior dog food will not contain these red-flag ingredients. Though high-quality dog foods can be a bit more expensive, the cost will be well worth it and may even save you money in vet bills in the long term by nourishing your Yorkipoo properly.

There has been a recent trend in grain-free dog food. Some claim that because wolves in the wild don't consume more than a trace amount of grains, domesticated dogs shouldn't either. The truth is that dogs are not genetically identical to wolves, and they have adapted to effectively utilize grains.

Grain-free dog food contains other plants instead of the grains. These are usually peas, lentils, potatoes, and legumes. These plant sources provide the starch to make the kibble and an added protein boost, allowing the manufacturer to cut back on more expensive animal proteins. This can lead to a depletion of the amino acid taurine. Taurine is found in animal proteins but not in plant proteins, and the FDA has linked this to a rise of cardiomyopathy in dogs who have been fed a grain-free diet. It is best to discuss with your vet what food is best for your Yorkipoo before following any food trend.

Categories of Dog Food

Commercial dog food comes in three basic categories: Puppy, Adult, and Senior. Knowing the difference between these three foods and choosing the right one is crucial for the health of your Yorkipoo.

Puppies, adult dogs, and senior dogs all have unique dietary needs. Puppies need more calories to support their growing bodies, as well as higher levels of protein and fat. Puppy food is formulated especially for dogs up to the age of 15 months, depending on the dog, taking into account the higher nutrient needs of a growing pup.

Adult dog food is formulated to satisfy the needs of a fully developed adult dog, typically 15 months and older. This food is not sufficient for a growing pup as it will not meet his nutritional needs.

Dog food formulated for senior dogs, typically around 11 years for a dog the size of the Yorkipoo, is both lower in calories and higher in fiber. This nutritional balance is made for senior dogs who may be a little less active than they once were. The lower caloric count can help counteract any weight gain in old age.

If you are choosing between quality commercial dog foods for your dog, make sure you choose the right one for his stage of development. If you aren't sure when to make the switch from one to the other, consult your vet for advice. Take into account your dog's lifestyle, activity level, and weight.

Homemade Dog Food

Some owners choose to skip commercial dog food altogether and make their dogs' meals themselves instead. This is the only real way to know exactly what your dog is eating. If you have the time and resources, homemade dog food can provide your Yorkipoo with a wonderful source of balanced nutrition, including real, whole foods and none of the preservatives

Photo Courtesy of Jen Berg

found in commercial foods. In addition, food cooked at home contains more nutrients than processed food. This is because the high temperature used during processing causes significant loss of nutrients.

Many homemade dog food recipes can be found online, but it's very important that you discuss specific recipes with your vet to be sure they provide your dog with all of the nutrients he needs. Individual breeds and even dogs of the same breed can have different nutritional needs. When making your dog's food yourself, it's important to get a professional opinion regarding ingredients and serving size.

Table Food – What Is Good, What Is Not

"Get yourself a magnetic list for your refrigerator which tells you safe human foods you can share and more importantly human foods that are deadly to your fur baby. Never feed your puppy anything unless you are certain it is safe and be sure to tell guests and children to never feed your fur baby human food unless they check with you first."

JENNIFER EMERT
Jen's Tiny Toys

When it comes to feeding your dog table food, the key to safety is knowing what is beneficial and what is not. In Chapter 3, we discussed a list of foods to never feed your Yorkipoo, so you may want to return there and refresh your memory before continuing on to this list of foods that are okay to share with your pup. Remember, feeding your dog directly from the table can quickly form bad habits such as begging. This may be cute the first time but will get old fast when you want to enjoy a meal in peace.

There are a number of things you can safely share with your dog from your kitchen as a special treat or snack, but remember that these should be given in moderation so that they don't upset the balance of your dog's nutrition. None of these items should be heavily seasoned, as this may cause your dog an upset stomach.

- White and brown rice
- Cooked eggs
- Oatmeal
- Carrots
- Cheese
- Peanut butter (without xylitol)
- Berries
- Green beans
- Seedless watermelon
- Bananas
- Peas
- Pineapple
- Apples
- Broccoli
- Potatoes

This is not a comprehensive list, and food sensitivities can differ from dog to dog, so consult your veterinarian if you think your Yorkipoo may have a food allergy or sensitivity.

Weight Management

If your Yorkipoo is overweight, you should deal with the problem immediately. Begin by implementing a more active routine. Consult Chapter 9 for ideas to make exercise fun for you and your dog. Also, consider where your dog is getting his nutrition. Is he eating a quality commercial food? Low-quality foods contain filler ingredients that will fill your dog up temporarily but don't provide adequate nutrients. Your dog may end up eating more of these foods to make up for the lack of nutrition, causing weight issues. If you prepare homemade dog food for your pup, you may need to go back to the vet or nutritionist to reevaluate ingredients and portion sizes.

Also, consider what your dog is eating when it isn't mealtime. Are you sharing too many snacks from the kitchen with your Yorkipoo? Moderation is the key to sharing special treats, and too many can be detrimental to your dog's health if it leads to obesity and disease. If weight is an issue for your dog, cut out the snacks and feed him only at designated mealtimes.

If you can't get your dog's weight under control by limiting snacks and providing a quality commercial food, discuss options with your vet. He or she may suggest a weight management food. These foods feature higher than average protein, lower than average fat, and fewer calories. These foods are formulated for adult dogs only and should never be given to a puppy. Remember to read food labels and choose a food made with high-quality ingredients.

CHAPTER 15
Dealing with Unwanted Behaviors

What Is Considered Bad Behavior?

Dog personalities vary as much as human personalities. No two are alike. We all want a well-trained, obedient dog, but even successful training won't keep a spunky dog from being spunky. Just like humans, dogs can exhibit behaviors that are annoying at times, but that doesn't necessarily mean they are bad. So, when it comes to bad habits and behaviors, what is and is not actually considered "bad"?

Barking – Barking is as natural for your dog as speaking is to you and should never be considered bad behavior. Yorkipoos can often be particularly chatty and bark a bit too frequently. Don't worry, there are measures you can take to correct the annoyance.

First, try to find the root cause of the barking. Is there a direct, consistent trigger such as seeing other people or dogs? If this is the case, socialization may be in order to give your dog a chance to engage with other pups and bark in an appropriate setting. If the problem is more sporadic and inconsistent, consider whether your Yorkipoo may simply be trying to get your attention. Are you spending enough one on one time with your dog? Yorkipoos have high social needs, and the barking issue may be a result of those needs not being met.

If your Yorkipoo has a problem with excessive barking, fill a soda bottle halfway with rocks or coins and shake it every time he barks. Tell him "quiet" in a calm voice and reward him with a small treat when he stops. Continue this method until he learns to be "quiet" on command.

Chasing – Some dogs are instinctually wired to chase things. While this behavior can

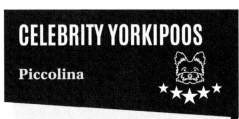

CELEBRITY YORKIPOOS

Piccolina

Piccolina is a Yorkipoo who was rescued from a shelter by Wags and Walks Rescue, a 501c3 dog rescue located in Los Angeles. Piccolina now lives a comfortable life with her mom in Newport Beach, California, and enjoys a following of over a thousand people on Instagram. You can see photos of her living in paradise on Instagram with the username @piccolinatheyorkiepoo.

Photo Courtesy
of Lori Duchak

become an issue, it should never be treated as "bad" behavior. Your dog is only doing what comes naturally to him. Obedience training can help this issue but may not eliminate it completely.

Digging – Much like chasing, digging is a natural behavior and may involve rolling around in the freshly disturbed dirt. This is not bad behavior, but it can become annoying and may be curbed with stricter supervision and obedience training.

Leash Pulling – This is a direct result of improper or inadequate training and is not bad behavior. Teach your dog the proper way to walk on a leash with the help of a trainer, and this annoyance can be eliminated altogether. While leash pulling from a dog as small as a Yorkipoo is not as dangerous as with other breeds, it should still be corrected right away.

Other unwanted behaviors that are not "bad" include chewing up toys or shoes, begging or stealing food, jumping on people, getting on furniture, and eating poop. All of these behaviors can be a nuisance but are typically not evidence of a poorly behaved dog.

Aggression – Behavior that should always be considered "bad" is any form of unprovoked aggression. This could be vicious growling, biting, lunging, or snarling. These behaviors are unacceptable, and if not dealt with immediately, they can result in serious injury or death for your dog or the object of his aggression. This includes food or possession aggression. There may be a root issue or trigger that you are not aware of, so consult a professional trainer or animal psychologist promptly if you are dealing with these truly bad and dangerous dog behaviors.

Finding the Root of the Problem

When dealing with any unwanted behavior, the first step to eliminating the issue is finding the root cause. Learning the why will make correcting the problem so much easier for both you and your dog.

Instinctual – If the unwanted behavior you are dealing with is something instinctually bred into your dog, it will probably be more difficult to correct. Try training with a professional, but if that doesn't work, you may have to redirect the unwanted behavior into an appropriate outlet. For example, if your dog loves to chase, find him a way to chase safely in a controlled environment. This applies to all instinctual issues, including chewing and digging. Allow your Yorkipoo to do these things in a way that is not inappropriate.

Lack of Training – The majority of a dog's unwanted behaviors stem from a simple lack of training. Leash tugging, jumping, begging for food, and jumping on furniture are all a direct result of inconsistent boundaries set by the owner. Training your dog consistently and purposefully is the best way

Photo Courtesy
of Robyn Cook

to correct these unwanted behaviors. See Chapter Ten for tips on where to get started.

If you are dealing with a real aggression issue with your dog, determine what the root cause might be. Could he be suffering from a health issue? Is there a traumatic event in your dog's past? A long-standing lack of socialization? If so, there may be a long road of recovery ahead for your Yorkipoo, and you will more than likely require the assistance of a trainer and possibly a dog psychologist. These behavioral issues can be a matter of life or death for a dog, so approach them with intention.

How to Properly Correct Your Dog

When it comes to correcting a dog, one thing is clear: punishment doesn't work. Unless your Yorkipoo has a deep-seated issue involving a traumatic past or a medical condition, he will generally want to please you with his actions. Correct him by showing him what you want him to do instead of the unwanted behavior. Revisit Chapter 10 for more information on positive reinforcement methods.

If it's an issue that does not concern safety, do your best to meet your dog in the middle with a solution that will make you both happy. If he loves to chew, keep a steady supply of interesting chew toys at his disposal so that he can still chew, but you don't have to worry about your belongings.

When to Call a Professional

Sometimes, even seemingly harmless unwanted behaviors can become a dangerous issue for your dog. Digging can be harmless if it only leads to a few holes in the backyard, but if it evolves into digging under the fence, it can become a serious problem quickly, exposing your dog to the many dangers that lie outside the fence. Likewise, losing a few pairs of shoes can be frustrating but not dangerous. However, if a chewer decides to eat a loose electrical cord or a toy with small batteries, it could end in an emergency trip to the animal hospital.

If your attempts to redirect your dog's behavior yourself have been futile, contact your local dog training facility and ask for help. They will undoubtedly have seen these issues before and will have the resources and tools to help you find a solution that works for you and your dog. It's important to seek help at the first sign of a problem and not let unwanted habits form. If you wait and habits do form, it will be much more challenging to correct the behavior down the road.

*Photo Courtesy
of Adele Meighan*

CHAPTER 16
Caring for Your Senior Yorkipoo

A Yorkipoo is considered "senior" around the age of 11. Caring for an aging dog can present a whole new set of challenges. Aging dogs, just like humans, typically require more medical care because they are prone to ailments such as arthritis, cognitive dysfunction, cataracts, hearing loss, incontinence, and the inability to regulate body temperature.

Photo Courtesy
of Tiffany Ferguson

Not all dogs reach this stage at the same time, and many can live comfortable and happy lives for years, even with these ailments. This chapter will discuss potential issues you may face with your aging dog and help you navigate the difficult end-of-life decisions when the time comes.

Common Old-Age Ailments

Arthritis – Osteoarthritis is a degenerative joint disease where the bones of a joint rub against each other due to the deterioration of the cartilage between them. This deterioration can cause severe pain, stiffness, and limited mobility. Osteoarthritis cannot be cured, but it can be treated with medication and supplements to slow the progression of the disease and treat symptoms.

Cataracts – Cataracts cause a dog to have blurry vision by creating an opacity in the normally clear lens. If your senior dog develops cataracts, have your vet monitor him closely for worsening symptoms. When left untreated, cataracts can sometimes lead to blindness. While this is not a death sentence for your Yorkipoo, it would be a major life adjustment for you and him. That said, many blind dogs live happy and healthy lives!

Cognitive Dysfunction – Senior dogs are susceptible to dementia, just like humans are. If you notice your dog forgetting something he does often or acting unusually out of his normal routine, discuss options with your vet for helping improve his quality of life. If your Yorkipoo experiences these symptoms, try to ease his frustration and confusion by making everyday tasks simpler for him. This could mean putting his food and water in a more visible place in the house, leading him outside more often or using a puppy pad to avoid accidents, and keeping his toys and belongings easily accessible.

Just like with humans, dogs with cognitive dysfunction can benefit greatly from mental stimulation. Continue to review and practice basic commands such as sit and stay with your senior dog or play a basic game of hide and seek with a toy. These activities can help to slow the worsening of this condition and can even help improve memory.

Hearing Loss – Hearing loss is common in old dogs. While many will lose some degree of hearing, they may not go completely deaf. Signs of hearing loss include a sudden lack of obedience, increased startle reaction, and excessive barking.

If your dog experiences hearing loss, you may need to find another form of communication. Teach your dog hand signals at the first sign of hearing loss so that if he loses his hearing completely, you can still communicate commands. It may also be helpful to keep a flashlight handy to signal for his attention.

Basic Senior Dog Care

When caring for your senior Yorkipoo, there are certain precautions you should take. Care for a senior dog should be focused on keeping him comfortable and happy. Like people, senior dogs have trouble regulating their body temperature. Be sure to provide your dog with extra warmth on a cold day and make sure he stays cool on a hot day.

Special accommodations may need to be made to make life more comfortable for your senior dog. If your dog has arthritis, he may benefit from a specially made bed to help with stiffness. If you have stairs, you may also need to consider keeping all of your dog's things on the lowest level of your home, so he doesn't need to climb the stairs.

Photo Courtesy
of Lori Duchak

As a dog ages, energy levels usually decline along with stamina. It's important that you still give your aging Yorkipoo regular, gentle exercise to keep him in shape. Obesity can be a problem in older dogs, who typically move around less, and it can exacerbate other age-related ailments such as arthritis and heart conditions. If obesity becomes a problem despite regular exercise, discuss options with your veterinarian. He or she may suggest switching to a different food.

Often, a dog's dental care is neglected throughout life, leading to potentially painful issues in old age. If your elderly dog suddenly seems to lose his appetite, check with your vet to see if the problem could be dental. Sometimes a painful tooth or painful gums can be enough to deter a dog from his dinner.

Your senior dog will probably need to see the vet more during his last years than he did previously. The AAHA (American Animal Hospital Association) recommends that you take your senior dog to the vet at least once every six months for a check-up. These regular vet visits can help you catch any conditions early and allow for more prompt treatment, potentially leading to a better quality of life for your Yorkipoo.

Illness and Injury Prevention

One of the most important aspects of senior dog care is preventing illness and injury. It's much more challenging for an elderly dog to overcome an illness or injury than it is for a younger dog.

As discussed above, exercise is just as important for a senior dog as it is for a young one. It should look a little different, though. Because a senior dog is more prone to injury, exercise should be done at a less vigorous pace that will have less impact on aging joints. Take your Yorkipoo for a nice, slow walk or take him for a swim. Avoid activities that involve jumping or climbing an incline. These activities may risk injury or aggravation of arthritis, causing your dog unnecessary pain.

Mental exercise is just as, if not more, important for a senior dog. Continue obedience training or practice into the senior years to keep his mind sharp and active. This may help prevent or slow cognitive decline.

To protect your senior dog from illness, be sure to continue his parasite medication for fleas and ticks. Also, make sure he stays up to date on his vaccinations. If an elderly dog does fall ill, he is more likely to suffer complications that may be life-threatening. A younger dog may contract the common Bordetella bacterium and suffer no real consequences, but for a senior dog, a simple infection can quickly turn into pneumonia, which may result in a hospital stay.

Photo Courtesy
of Jen Berg

Supplements and Nutrition

Proper nutrition, including supplementation, is more important than ever when a dog reaches his final years. Quality of life and severity of geriatric conditions can be greatly influenced by nutrition. There are many supplements on the market that are specifically formulated for senior dogs.

Before adding any supplement to your dog's diet, consult your veterinarian. He or she may be able to direct you to a quality brand or alert you to possible side effects or interactions with your dog's current medications.

Below is a list of the most common supplements.

Glucosamine and Chondroitin – Two supplements often paired together to combat osteoarthritis, glucosamine and chondroitin have been found to be therapeutic in the treatment of canine arthritis. These compounds are found naturally in cartilage and are made by the body.

When looking for a glucosamine and chondroitin supplement, look for highly reputable brands that source all of their ingredients from the United States. Imported glucosamine has been found to contain many contaminants, including lead, especially when sourced from China. Since the FDA does not regulate supplements, the only way to know if you are getting a quality product is to be vigilant and diligent in your research. Even popular pet store brands that say "made in the USA" can include ingredients sourced from China.

Omega-3 Fatty Acids – Omega-3 fatty acids like DHA and EPA have been shown to be beneficial in many ways that may benefit your senior dog. These fatty acids are beneficial for the brain, potentially improving cognitive function in old age and may even give your Yorkipoo's immune system a boost. According to the American Kennel Club, "The addition of omega-3 to the diet may [also] help reduce inflammation and can promote cell membrane health."

Antioxidants – Including an extra source of antioxidants in your senior dog's diet can be beneficial as well. You can do this by purchasing a supplement or by simply allowing your dog to snack on high antioxidant fruits such as berries and apples.

Probiotics – Probiotics help maintain healthy bacteria in the gut, the place where up to 80 percent of a dog's immune defenses reside. This can improve immune function and help your senior dog ward off illness and disease more efficiently.

When It's Time to Say Goodbye

Undoubtedly, the hardest part of being a pet owner is knowing when it's time to say goodbye. Our dogs devote the best years of their life to us, unconditionally gifting us with love and loyalty, no matter the circumstances. When you see that your beloved Yorkipoo is experiencing more pain than joy, it may be time to consider the most difficult decision you will face in pet ownership.

Many people believe that it is one of the toughest and greatest responsibilities of animal ownership to know when to humanely relieve an animal from the pain when the end of the animal's life is inevitable. It is never an easy decision and often leads to an array of emotions for the owner, including sorrow, guilt, and second thoughts.

How Will You Know When the Time Is Right?

No one knows your dog better than you do, and no one will be able to make this decision for you. You and your Yorkipoo have a bond that nobody else can understand, and that is exactly what makes you the right person to make the final call. If you have a gut feeling that your senior dog has had a sharp decline in health and is hurting more than he is enjoying life, talk to your vet. It may be time to say goodbye. A few telltale signs that death is imminent are extreme lethargy, lack of interest in anything, loss of coordination, incontinence, and not eating or drinking.

Only you and your dog will know when this time is. Your dog has trusted you with his life during all the time you spent together, and he trusts you with it now. If you believe putting him down humanely will end his suffering, speak to your vet and discuss euthanasia.

Once you have made the decision that the time has come to humanely end your dog's suffering, understand that second thoughts are normal. Don't second-guess the decision that is best for your dog just because it's hard for you. Grieving over this decision is natural and normal. Talk to a trusted friend or family member to help you cope during this difficult time.

Once you have made the decision, as long as the vet agrees that death is inevitable, the process happens fairly quickly. The point is to end your dog's suffering, so there is no sense in putting it off for a few days.

The Euthanasia Process

Before you take your dog to the vet, call any friends or family members who may want to say goodbye. Some vets also offer to come to your home and perform the euthanasia there, in order to make the process easier for your dog. Either way, you will have the option to be present when the vet performs the procedure. Although it may be hard for you to watch your dog die, know that it will bring your dog comfort and peace in his last moments if you are there with him, holding him and comforting him.

During the procedure, your vet will administer a solution, typically phenobarbital, intravenously. The solution is usually thick with a blue, pink, or purple tint. The vet may inject it directly into a vein or into an intravenous catheter. Once the solution is injected, it will quickly travel through your dog's body, causing him to lose consciousness within just a few seconds. Your Yorkipoo will feel no pain. Breathing will slow and then stop altogether. Cardiac arrest will occur and cause death within thirty seconds of the injection.

Your vet will check for signs of life and will most likely step out of the room for a few moments to give you time to say a final goodbye. Your vet and the office staff have been through this before and will understand the emotional weight of the situation for you. They should provide you with privacy and be a source of comfort if needed. Be sure to make payments and after-death arrangements beforehand so that you don't have to deal with it after.

Your dog's body may still move after death, so don't be alarmed if you see twitching. He may also release bodily fluids, and this is also normal.

If you have chosen to have your dog cremated, your vet will coordinate with a cremation service and notify you when your Yorkipoo's ashes are ready. If you are taking your deceased dog home for burial, the vet will place your dog's remains in a container and will typically carry it out to the car for you. Burying your beloved pet at home is legal in most states, but not all. If this is your plan, check your local laws ahead of time so that you are fully prepared on this difficult day.

Whichever you choose, once you leave the vet's office you will begin the grieving process, remembering that the love and bond you and your Yorkipoo shared will always be in your memory and in your heart.

Printed in Great Britain
by Amazon

46222428R10079